FREEDOM TO KNOW
A Background Book

FREEDOM TO KNOW
A Background Book

by JOSEPH CARTER

Parents' Magazine Press
New York

Each Background Book is concerned with the broad spectrum of people, places, and events affecting the national and international scene. Written simply and clearly, the books in the series will engage the minds and interest of people living in a world of great change.

Library of Congress Cataloging in Publication Data

Carter, Joseph.
    Freedom to know; a background book.
    SUMMARY: Examines the issue of censorship and freedom of information in their legal and social aspects.
    Includes bibliographical references.
    1. Freedom of information—United States. 2. Freedom of information. I. Title.
JC599.U5C357   323.44'5'0973   74-4433
ISBN 0-8193-0738-6
ISBN 0-8193-0739-4 (lib. bdg.)

CONTENTS

PREFACE

THIS BOOK IS predicated on the belief that most men and women—certainly most *young* men and women—are interested and concerned about the world in which they live.

It is obviously impossible to function today, as a living and useful person, without knowing what is happening in this world.

Today, the problem of knowing is far more difficult and complicated than it ever has been before in the history of the world.

Scientists point out that of all the scientists who have existed since the beginning of history, 90 percent are now living, and that forty thousand words a day are added to the world's scientific knowledge.

Much the same is true in other fields of knowledge, and especially in the fields of government and politics. When the United Nations was founded in 1945, for example, the representatives of 50 nations signed the charter. Today there are more than 135 member nations, the majority of which, only a generation ago, did not exist as separate entities.

The world today is in the midst of such a turmoil of political change as has not been known since half the ruling empires of Europe were destroyed by World War I.

Today's younger generation, then, is faced with an explosion of change and knowledge that their fathers never dreamed of; and yet, basically, all the information about it comes through the media of communications. All that anyone can learn of this new world is through reading newspapers, magazines, and books, listening to radio, or watching television.

Communications itself is undergoing its own revolution, symbolized perhaps by television but including a whole range of inventions that can only be regarded with awe when it is considered in how few years they have been perfected: the tape recorder, ultra-high-frequency radio and television transmission systems, communications satellites, high-speed teleprinters, telephone cables that carry two hundred messages simultaneously.

In this veritable flood, how is the concerned individual to judge the accuracy of the information he receives?

This book was written with the hope of giving the reader some general guidelines as to how to go about this: partly to attempt to show the reader the strengths and weaknesses of the various media and the eternal conflict between the press and government on the limits of freedom of information, but mostly to illustrate how vital for everyone alive today is this freedom of information, or the freedom to know.

Two points are made clear in the book, but should be emphasized in advance. First: the term "media" is used to include all forms of communication—books, magazines, newspapers, radio, television, or any other way in which information is communicated—and, unless "newspapers" or "news magazines" are specified, the term "press representatives" is used as a generic term to include reporters for radio and television stations. Second: there is a clear distinction between "freedom of the press" and "freedom of information," or "the freedom to know." The battle for freedom of the press was waged by earlier men for at least three hundred years but now, at least in democratic countries, it seems safely won.

The battle for the freedom to know, however, seems to have just begun.

1

A CONTEMPORARY CONCEPT–AND ITS ANCIENT ROOTS

FREEDOM OF THE PRESS may be defined as the right of the press to publish information of public interest within the limitations of the laws relating to security of the state, libel, and obscenity, *without the prior permission of the government.*

Freedom of information or the freedom to know concerns itself with the proper limitations of those laws. In other words, what information should be published in the public interest, and what may be kept secret in the interest of the security of the state? What are the boundaries of libel and obscenity?

The politico-technological revolution of the last ten years touched upon in the preface has been accompanied by an ideological revolution that is not only questioning but very obviously changing the previous definitions of security and of libel and obscenity.

What is the responsibility of the press in the midst of this revolution?

What is the responsibility of government?

To confine the issue for the moment to the security of the state, it is notable that when Henry Kissinger was in the process of becoming Secretary of State, he made much of his intention to conduct foreign affairs more openly than in the past, to the vast approval of newsmen and many members of Congress—a clear indication of his understanding of the changing times.[1]

But the key part of his statement, as far as the public is concerned, was the phrase "more openly," for no one knows better than Kissinger that completely open discussion of serious international affairs, as he amply demonstrated and frequently explained during his long and laborious negotiations to achieve a cease-fire in Vietnam, is impossible.

But how much of these serious negotiations are properly kept secret, and who is to make the decisions on whether to or not?

There are no definite answers to most of these questions for the very good reason that no one person has a completely satisfactory answer.

What we are seeing today is a whole new approach being worked out, based on this new concept of freedom of information. Eventually it will be worked out, as so many developments in American history have been, only after endless analysis and debate, trial and error, and power struggles between the government and the press.

Freedom of the press for more than two centuries has been recognized as one of the most important freedoms of any democratic society. Other freedoms—freedom of religion and of peaceable assembly—are of almost equally basic importance, but reflection will show that without freedom of the press it is unlikely that the other two would long endure.

Certainly the Founding Fathers were most conscious of freedom of the press, since it is incorporated in the First Amendment to the Constitution. Jefferson himself wrote: "Were it left to me to decide whether we should have a government without newspapers or newspapers without government, I should not hesitate a moment to prefer the latter." [2]

And, contrariwise, it is necessary to reflect only on the complete control that totalitarian governments around the world maintain over the dissemination of information to realize its importance to a democracy. The attitude of the dictators was succinctly put by Lenin:

"Why should freedom of speech and freedom of press be allowed? Why should a government which is doing what it believes to be right allow itself to be criticized? Why should any man be allowed to buy a printing press and disseminate pernicious opinions calculated to embarrass the government?" [3]

Even when dictators apparently encourage free discussion of faults in the government, prudent men tread warily. For eighteen months, from January 1956 to June 1957, the leaders of mainland China—Chou En-Lai and Mao Tse-Tung—publicly and repeatedly invited criticism of the regime and the slogan, "Let a hundred flowers bloom and diverse schools of thought contend," became familiar even in the West. The controlled Chinese press was flooded with letters. In June 1957 the government, obviously seriously disturbed at the volume of criticism, suddenly cracked down. A number of the more prominent critics were executed, some disappeared, others were imprisoned, and still others were forced to publicly recant their words.[4]

At the present time, in no country ruled by a dictator (China and Russia, many of the nations of Africa and Latin America, the Philippines, and to a large extent Greece, Spain, and Portugal) is the dissemination of news critical of the government permitted. Indeed, most of these nations require that news be presented in such a way as to support in a positive fashion the government's position, whatever it may be.

But even in the democracies, governments are most sensitive to what the press has to say about them and are constantly locked in greater or lesser struggles with the press, as recent events in the United States alone have dramatically illustrated. The difference is that democracies do not control the press. They do not arbitrarily close down papers, or appoint editors. While the United States is the center of our attention, it is well not to forget that similar, though less spectacular government–press struggles have been going on in Great Britain, in West Germany, and in France.

The reason for these struggles, the reason why *all* governments are so concerned about the press, lies in one simple word: Power.

Through all the millennia of recorded history until comparatively recent times, information was jealously guarded by the ruling classes—the prerogative of the priests, the conquerors, the dictators.

An example is found in the reign of Amenemhet III, a pharaoh of Egypt (c. 1849–1801 B.C.).

Almost more than it is today, the Nile then was the lifeline of Egypt; on its waters depended the entire economy of the country. In times of low water, there was apt to be drought and famine; in times of high water, there could be flooding and famine. The southern frontier of Egypt then was near Wadi Halfa, which is located close beside the so-called Second Cataract of the river, about 600 miles upstream from Cairo. To protect the frontier, an earlier pharaoh had constructed twin forts called Semneh and Kummeh, one on each side of the river at Wadi Halfa.

At Semneh, Amenemhet III ordered that the garrison engrave on rocks in the cataract the levels of the water as it rose and fell; still later, stone markers were erected at points along the banks of the river to enable the Egyptians to plot the movement of the water volume in greater detail. These markers are now called nilometers. (The engravings are still visible and some of the original markers are still standing.)

Amenemhet ended up with two benefits from this system, one of the utmost practical importance and one more nebulous but possibly of almost equal value.

First, he had advance information on the amount of water that his farmers would receive for the irrigation of their crops, and so could judge whether the harvest would be plentiful or sparse. This was important not only for the food supply, but also for the taxation system on which his entire regime depended. In years of plenty, the tax on individual crops was small; in years of scarcity, it was increased.

The second benefit came from the fact that the common people of the Nile delta had, of course, no inkling of how Amenemhet got his information, since it was conveyed to him from Semneh by courier. To them, Amenemhet seemed indeed a descendant of the gods, able to foretell the rise and fall of the Nile with uncanny accuracy.

There are countless examples through history of the value of information to those who control it; of military campaigns won or lost because of the control of information. Waterloo was lost in a maze of misinformation. Empires were made and lost through control of information, from Caesar to Hitler.

But all through the centuries of history in which leaders have jealously guarded the sources of information, ordinary people have had the entirely human desire to want to know.

"It is the greatest pleasure of the Athenians," Demosthenes tells us, "to wander through the streets asking, 'What is the news?' " All civilizations and all rulers have recognized that fact.[5]

What may be called the first newspaper long antedated the invention of the printing press. It was the *Acta Diurna* (*Daily Chronicle* is a fairly accurate translation) that Julius Caesar established in ancient Rome. The ability to read, in those days, was pretty much confined to the upper classes, though there were many exceptions. In some enlightened households, for example, slaves were taught to read, and some teachers took it upon themselves to teach the proletarii, the lowest class of citizens, to read. Conversely, some generals who had achieved high rank only through fighting ability were unable to read and bought slaves solely for their ability to do so.

At any rate, the circulation of the *Acta Diurna* was at first restricted to the top officials of the government and of the military, and its news was restricted to the publication of royal decrees, victories won on the field of battle, and so on.

Later, personal news of high-born individuals—marriages, births, deaths, for example—was added.

Caesar finally ordered that the *Acta Diurna* be posted in public places. Here the local populace would gather, and one who could read would read the paper aloud. The modern equivalent of this is found in the thousands of tiny, poverty-stricken villages around the world—some even in states as advanced as Italy, Greece, and Turkey—where there is only one radio for the entire populace. This radio is set up in the village square and the townspeople gather to listen to it. In the United States, even as late as the 1930s, when radios were relatively new, when an event as important as the World Series was on, radio stores would connect a radio to a loudspeaker on the sidewalk outside and fans by the hundreds would gather to listen to the play-by-play. The same is true today with television sets, as witness the gatherings in front of any television display window during an interesting event.

Caesar noted the avidity of the people for news, and to the official reports he ordered items of popular interest to be added—stories about weather conditions and floods, about fires and street stabbings, about what was in supply at the various food markets around the city. In short, the essence of the modern newspaper—except no speculation about what Pompey or Scipio might be up to!

But the thought that the public had a right to this

information would have been as alien to Caesar as the thought of flying to the moon; the thought that *anyone* had the right to question his actions would have struck him as sheer lunacy.

Indeed, it needed some sixteen hundred years before there was even to be a serious challenge to the theory that the government was the sole owner and proprietor of news and that news should be allowed to be printed without the *prior* approval of the government. Even then, no claim was made for freedom of information. The concern was solely with freedom of the press.

It had taken all those centuries, and the vast changes in human concepts and human institutions that occurred during them, to establish an intellectual atmosphere in which the notion of freedom of the press could even be conceived.

The empires of ancient Rome had long since vanished; the Age of Feudalism had reached its zenith and was disappearing; even the Renaissance had already seen its greatest glory. But the Dark Ages and the Renaissance had witnessed the emergence of a powerful new intellectual force that was to challenge and finally break the autocratic intellectual authority of the church: the university.

Some of the western world's most distinguished universities were born during the Dark Ages—notably the University of Paris, which became the model for half the universities of Europe, from Oxford to Leipzig—but, still, during the Dark Ages these universities had devoted most of their intellectual energies to debating the finer points of theology.

It remained for the Renaissance, with its sudden upsurge of human knowledge, particularly in the sciences, to inspire the universities to deal with the entire human condition rather than simply the spiritual. It is impossible to imagine, for example, another Leonardo living in the twelfth rather than the fifteenth century, making detailed sketches of the human anatomy from cadavers.

It was the universities of Italy, where the Renaissance reached its earliest and finest flower, that first broke the medieval mold, and thus became, in their day, the most renowned universities of Europe. The most noted scholars of the entire western world vied for appointment to their faculties. In his monumental *Renaissance in Italy*, John Addington Symonds describes how, in 1224, the University of Bologna, with ten thousand students, was powerful enough to successfully defy an order by Emperor Frederick II that it close; how the city of Florence "engaged the best teachers and did not hesitate to devote a yearly sum of 2,500 golden florins to the maintenance of their . . . school." [6]

This spirit of intellectual freedom moved northward, as did the spirit of the entire Renaissance, first to France and then to the Low Countries; finally to England and Germany.

In the midst of all this intellectual ferment came a practical invention that was to be the most important breakthrough in communication since the invention of the alphabet: the printing press. Johann Gutenberg invented the printing press. Or, more precisely, Gutenberg invented movable type.

For the world then, and the world now, it was certainly an invention even more important than television.

Try to imagine the difference. Before Gutenberg, books had been printed by a system called "block printing." This method consisted of an experienced carver taking a block of wood the size of the page to be printed, and carving onto it all the words of that page of the book. It was Gutenberg's genius to decide to make metal molds of each of the letters of the alphabet separately so that they could be combined to make up any word, sentence, or page. Again, imagine the difference. Previously, by the block system, it would take an experienced carver as much as a week to do one page. With movable type, it could be done in a matter of hours. Besides, from metal letters, many more impressions could be made.

Books which previously had taken years to produce, one by one, could now be turned out in a few months, and in far greater volume.

It was against this background of both intellectual questing and technological revolution that the first real demand for freedom of the press was made.

It came about in an odd way and from a possibly unexpected man: the poet John Milton.

Milton, besides being the greatest poet of his age, was also a leading figure in the fight to reform the Church of England, a cabinet minister to Oliver Cromwell, a political figure of considerable importance—and he was unhappily married. He was thirty-five and he married a girl of seventeen. Whether it was due to the difference in age or not, their relationship became so insupportable that she finally left him. Milton was not insensitive to her position; in fact, he wrote a pamphlet arguing that the religious sanctity of marriage was simply a clerical dogma, not a divine law of God, and that if two married persons found themselves to be of totally incompatible character, they should be allowed to divorce.

Two things about the pamphlet combined to raise a furor of almost unprecedented dimensions in England: first, to argue that divorce be granted on the mere grounds of incompatibility in England in 1643 was nothing short of heresy; second, the pamphlet had been issued without a license from the Stationers' Company—the official government agency to which all manuscripts were required to be submitted *before* publication.

Then, the following year, to compound his felony, Milton issued—also without a license—what is without doubt his most famous piece of prose writing. It bore the formidable title of *Areopagitica, a speech of Mr. John*

Milton for the Liberty of Unlicensed Printing, to the Parliament of England.

The Stationers' Company petitioned the House of Lords to try Milton for his deliberate flouting of the law, but by now the winds of intellectual freedom had risen enough in England so that, while the Parliament did not repeal the licensing laws, it never brought Milton to trial, thus, in effect, condoning printing without a pre-granted license.[7]

The next important case concerning freedom of the press occured in the Colonies, in New York in 1735, and involved Peter Zenger, an immigrant printer who published the *New York Weekly Journal.* Zenger's trial is now regarded as one of the great steps forward in the development of freedom of the press.[8]

Zenger had published a series of articles savagely critical of the policies of the then Crown Governor of New York, William Cosby. Zenger was charged with libel, was arrested, thrown into jail, and brought to trial.

The charge against Zenger was libel, the legal definition of which is that statements known to be false and defamatory may not be published. Zenger's defense lawyer, a Philadelphia attorney named Andrew Hamilton, did not question the libel law itself, nor did he argue that the articles Zenger had printed were or were not libelous. What he *did* argue was that it was up to the jury to decide whether the articles constituted libel, while the attorney for the Crown argued that the

jury had only the right to determine whether Zenger
had, in fact, published the articles. The judge would
then decide whether they constituted libel.

Zenger was, of course, acquitted. One important
point established at his trial was that it was up to the
people of a state, as represented by the jury, to
determine whether the plaintiff (in this case, Cosby)
had been libeled; it would not be left to the state, as
represented by the Crown-appointed judge, to make
the determination. A second important point Hamilton made was that the statements printed by Zenger
were true: in other words, that truth is, per se, a
defense against libel.

When it came to the writing of the Constitution, the
men who framed it—most of whom were among the
most learned and well informed in the world, familiar
with the writings and thinking of Milton, John Locke,
and a host of other humanist thinkers and philoso-
phers—were obviously perfectly aware of the implications of the Zenger case.

In addition, the Founding Fathers were men of
intense practicality and, faced with formulating the
world's first written Constitution, they knew that if the
document was to endure as the governmental frame-
work for a new nation, it could not possibly take into
account all the contingencies of the future. They
therefore decided to confine themselves to stating what
they felt to be basic principles. That is why our
Constitution is the shortest of all national Constitutions
and why men today sometimes complain that it is too

ambiguous and wish that the Founding Fathers had been a little more specific. Our definition of freedom of the press, for example, says only: "Congress shall make no law . . . abridging the freedom . . . of the press."

That's all there is.

Nothing at all about what may or may not be published. It would, indeed, be perfectly lawful for a newspaper to advocate the overthrow of the government, provided that it did not advocate the use of arms to do so.

Freedom of the press to print what it deems correct, therefore, is quite secure.

Today's issue of freedom of information is quite a different topic.

There is nothing in the Constitution and no law that requires the government to *supply* information either to individual citizens or the press. The only requirement is listed in the Constitution among the duties of the President: "He shall from time to time give to the Congress Information of the State of the Union . . ."

The issue today is basically this: how much control should the government have over information that it would prefer to keep to itself?

To put it in its simplest terms, should the government have the right to enjoin newspapers from printing such information as the "Pentagon Papers" contain, and should it have the right to send a reporter to jail for refusing to reveal the sources from which he receives information?

"Paramount among the responsibilities of a free

press is the duty to prevent any part of the Government from deceiving the people," wrote the late Supreme Court Justice Hugo Black in his concurring opinion in the "Pentagon Papers" case. Since the Supreme Court ruled in favor of the press on this important occasion, it would seem that the issue had been resolved.[9]

But that is not so, and it requires only the briefest of glances at the problems involved to see why. It also shows why the right of freedom of information is so tangled an area that the battles around it will continue for generations to come, just as generations past fought for the freedom of the press.

Not even the most extreme proponents of full freedom of information have ever argued that the government should provide free access of information on purely military matters. In time of war, or even undeclared war such as Vietnam and Korea, it is obvious that advance disclosure of troop operations, for example, would cost the needless loss of American lives. The enemy would simply be lying in wait. Similarly with ship and convoy movements or aircraft deployment.

Instantly, the problem becomes complicated because it becomes only fair to ask: What about the secret bombing of Cambodia? The military still insist that the bombing was necessary to forward military objectives, which is presumably true, or at least a statement presumably made in good faith from a purely military point of view. Yet members of both houses of Congress insist that the military kept the bombings secret ("lied about them," is the even stronger accusation) because it knew that if the news became public, Congress might well forbid the bombings. The bombings were, these congressional members insist, an unwarranted extension of the American role in the war in Southeast Asia.

It is extremely improbable that, in the event of a major conflict, there would be any right to information about purely military operations, and past history has shown that the public itself resents not the fact that such information is kept secret, but any part of the press that prints such information.

In diplomatic affairs, too, the government is generally conceded the right to secrecy under certain circumstances. The negotiations between Henry Kissinger and Le Duc Tho, chief negotiator for North Vietnam, were conducted in an atmosphere of almost complete secrecy. It is true that the newspapers reported that the negotiations were in progress, but the substance of the negotiations—and in some cases even the meeting place itself—were not known until the final, public announcement that a truce had been achieved.

The need for this secrecy is as obvious as the need for military secrecy. Two points may prove the validity of that statement.

First, while diplomatic negotiations may be conducted in secrecy, they are not conducted in a vacuum

without regard for the political considerations implicit
in them. There is no doubt that, during the Vietnam
negotiations, there were political groups in both North
Vietnam and in the United States that would not be
satisfied with the terms of any truce. In North
Vietnam, experienced observers believe, there were
those who felt that since the United States was
withdrawing its military forces there was no need to
make any concessions whatever; in the United States
there were those who felt that any further concessions
to North Vietnam would be a betrayal of the nearly
fifty thousand Americans who had been killed there. It
is impossible to believe that either of these groups had
the political strength to halt the negotiations, but it is
certain that a day-by-day reporting of the negotiations
would have allowed them to muster what political
opposition they could, and this in turn could have
protracted the negotiations for months. In the hard
reality of conducting negotiations, a diplomat is given
his mission within the limits of what, at best, would be
the terms his country would like to get or, at worst,
what are the absolute minimum of terms his country
will settle for. The final terms arrived at are up to his
skill as a negotiator. The handicap that would be
imposed upon him if every concession he agreed to was
blazoned forth in the newspapers is obvious.

Second, since in diplomatic negotiations each side
wants to achieve the terms most advantageous to itself,
for one side to know in advance the limits of the terms

of the other side would give it an enormous advantage. That is why the Administration said that those congressmen who proposed setting an arbitrary deadline for the removal of troops from South Vietnam were in effect proposing to deal the North Vietnamese the ace of trumps. How would any negotiator react if he knew that the opposite side was under a mandate to reach a settlement by such-and-such a date? Stall, obviously. Wait until the opposite side was under such pressure to obtain a settlement that it would be prepared to cede almost anything. A perfect example of this is embodied in a story published in *The New York Times* on July 23, 1971. The article was written by William Beecher, then the *Times*'s Pentagon reporter, later Deputy Assistant Secretary of Defense. It spelled out the United States "fall-back" position (i.e., the absolute minimum of the terms this country would settle for) in the Strategic Arms Limitation Talks in Helsinki, then also being conducted by Kissinger. According to other members of the U.S. negotiating team, the American position was compromised to the extent that there was serious consideration given to simply breaking off the talks and, according to the *Times*, Kissinger was so outraged that he flew back to the United States and "literally pounded the President's table" in rage over the leak.

The moment all this has been said about the need for secrecy, military and diplomatic, the opposite side of the coin turns up.

What may *not* properly be justified as secret in these fields?

For one thing, military mistakes.

Military men are, by and large, no different from other men in positions of power. Some are men of complete integrity and great intelligence utterly dedicated to their sworn duty, the defense of the Republic; some are the opposite, venal and without wit, and there are those who combine the opposites of those qualities. But the great majority fall, as with most men, somewhere in between, of greater or lesser honesty and brain power. Even the best of men, however, can make mistakes, and only the most extreme proponents of the right to secrecy have ever argued that their mistakes should not be made public.

In fact, the histories of war show that it is not only impossible to conceal mistakes, but even mischances due to circumstances over which the commander had no control. Military historians, for example, are still arguing how the Battle of Waterloo might have turned out if Marshal Ney had engaged the forces of Wellington, as Napoleon had ordered him to do. "Ney has ruined France," [10] said Napoleon, with considerable justification. Or whether the Civil War might have ended in July 1864 if General Burnside had been able to get his troops through the gap in the Confederate fortifications at Petersburg, as Grant wanted him to.

But mistakes on the battlefield have never been regarded as coming under the cloak of government secrecy. For one thing, usually too many people are involved, and too many insistent reporters inquire into the operations afterward. And in today's world, mistakes and misdeeds come to light much more quickly. It may have taken almost three years for the heinous massacre at My Lai to come to the attention of the American people, but it took nearly three generations for the equally heinous massacre at Wounded Knee to be generally known.

It is in the non-combat sections of military operations that the question of concealment of information arises far more frequently. From the "rotten beef" scandals of the Civil War to the fraudulent materiel procurement investigations of World War II, those involved naturally would like the cloak of official secrecy to conceal their criminal activities, exactly as a crooked mayor or a larcenous city official wants the shield of the closed session to conceal his action. The claim of the right to secrecy here is obviously preposterous.

The question of proper governmental concealment of information has long been an especially murky one, and offers an almost perfect case-book example of why it is impossible to write a set of hard-and-fast rules. In almost all such cases it is men and motives, the circumstances and the times, that determine the rightness or wrongness of the concealment.

Consider the words of Franklin D. Roosevelt when, in his campaign for the presidency in 1940, he gave the mothers and fathers of America the assurance again and again and again: "Your boys are not going to be sent into any foreign wars." [11]

Could not President Roosevelt be accused of deceiving the people? His assurance was delivered barely six months after the fall of France, and while the Battle of Britain was being waged. The Nazi air force was subjecting England to the heaviest aerial bombardment the world had ever seen up to that time, and Roosevelt already knew that unless the United States intervened, Germany would win the war.

Only six weeks after the election, in one of his Fireside Chats, Roosevelt was pledging the United States to become the "great arsenal of democracy," telling the nation that "a nation can have peace with the Nazis only at the price of total surrender. . . . All of us, in the Americas, would be living at the point of a Nazi gun . . ." Even during the campaign, in secret negotiations announced to the Congress later as an accomplished fact, Roosevelt arranged the transfer of fifty over-age destroyers to England in return for leases to build American bases in eight British possessions in the western Atlantic Ocean. The announcement of this transfer came almost three months to the day after Congress had passed an amendment to the Naval Appropriations Bill providing that the United States could transfer *no* items of military equipment to *any* foreign government unless the chiefs of staff of the army or the navy certified that the items were useless for the defense of the United States.

Could not Roosevelt be accused not only of deceiving the American people, but also the U.S. Congress? There were plenty who did accuse him, even then.

It is easy to forget now the strength of American sentiment against entering World War II—until Pearl Harbor. A Roper poll taken shortly after Germany attacked Poland showed that 67.4 percent of the American people favored staying out of the war—an anti-war sentiment far higher than the highest against the Vietnam War—and when the extension of the Selective Service Act came up in Congress in August 1941 (four months before America would be at war) it was passed in the House of Representatives by a margin of *one* vote.

It may be useful to keep in mind that the anti-war sentiment had four major bases of support: the "America Firsters" who believed that America should steer clear of all foreign entanglements; the pacifists; those who had witnessed the Senate hearings presided over by Gerald P. Nye of Wisconsin during the mid-1920s into the profits of the munitions makers in World War I; and those who resented the fact that political cartoonists in many European papers were fond of depicting Uncle Sam as "Uncle Shylock" for suggesting that it was about time to collect the loans that had been made during World War I to European governments. But their collective voices, loud and clear until December 7, 1941, were suddenly muted.

Pearl Harbor solved all of Roosevelt's problems on that score.

During and after World War II, therefore, those
who would have liked to accuse Roosevelt of deceiving
the American people were an insignificant minority.
No Supreme Court decision was ever required on any
of his military policies.

If it be argued that all this is past history, it is well to
remember Santayana's much-quoted remark: "Those
who cannot remember the past are condemned to
repeat it." [12]

It is apparent now that in the quest for the most
complete freedom of information possible, two factors
of today's world emerge as the most compelling: the
vast, almost bewildering array of scientific devices
evolved in the field of communications within the past
few years, plus the great new spirit of inquiry that has
emerged in this country in only the last decade. The
second is, of course, by far the more important, since
without the spirit of inquiry, without the drive to get
behind official explanations of official actions, the
electronic devices would remain only machines.

2

THE TORRENT OF
INFORMATION—AND
HOW TO DETERMINE
THE TRUTH

IT IS POSSIBLE that the average person has not yet
realized the magnitude of the communications revolution, for it is a quality of the human mind that it
cannot really grasp what it has not experienced. The
latest census, for example, shows that there are twenty
million people in the United States who are sixty-five
or older; in their childhood, therefore, the automobile
must have been very much of a rarity. Undoubtedly,
the image of a nation of horse-drawn vehicles and
bicycles is very real and vivid to them, yet the majority
of the population, born in later years, while it may
every now and then try to *imagine* what the country
was like back then, does not really grasp it any more

than we today can really grasp what it must be like to walk on the moon, or to live in a world without television.

The new media are the basic factor in that electronic revolution that is giving the average citizen today so much more information than even his father had. It is highly unlikely that the father, in his youth, had ever seen the inside of a Senate hearing room; yet almost everyone who has looked at television within the past ten years has seen one.

The question is: what does the average citizen do with this enormous amount of information available to him? No one can answer that at the moment, of course, and there are still countless routine governmental actions and operations that never reach the headlines nor appear on television, but by and large, today's citizen can hardly make a justifiable complaint that the communications media fail to inform him of important developments. It is all there for the reading, or the viewing.

One area in which it is obviously unlikely, as Kissinger hinted, that the average person will be completely informed is that of the progress of international negotiations, and the reason for that can best be illustrated by citing a case of actual complicated and danger-laden negotiations in the immediate past: President John F. Kennedy's actions in the Cuban missile crisis of 1962.

It would be more contemporary to deal with a later

case such as Kissinger's handling of the Vietnam or Middle East negotiations, but until Kissinger writes his own account of them or some other chief negotiator feels that enough time has elapsed to be able to consider them as a part of history, that is impossible.

The Cuban crisis is the most recent on which we have fairly complete information and which illustrates what information the public received—and when.

The most striking phase of the background to these negotiations—from the point of view solely of the right of information—is the sheer sum of information that a President must consider in a situation that, if mishandled, could conceivably lead to a world war.

In 1962, the "Cold War" relationship between the United States and the Soviet Union had reached a point of extreme tension; only two years earlier, a projected "summit conference" between President Dwight D. Eisenhower and the Soviet Premier, Nikita Khrushchev, had been called off because an American high altitude U-2 reconnaissance aircraft had been shot down over Russia while making aerial photographs for military purposes. Some international observers were openly speculating on whether a war between the super-powers could be avoided. American and Russian interests seemed to be in conflict all around the world: in Europe, in the Middle East, in Africa, in South America. It appeared that one wrong action, one mistake of judgment on either side, might result in World War III.

Fidel Castro had toppled the military dictatorship of Fulgencio Batista in Cuba on New Year's Day, 1959. Openly proclaiming himself a Marxist and a revolutionary, denouncing "Yankee imperialism," Castro had nonetheless made a trip to the United States in May 1959 seeking United States aid for his new regime; it is to the discredit of the Eisenhower administration and of the then Secretary of State, John Foster Dulles, that it was refused. Castro, whose entire economy depended upon sugar, turned to the USSR for economic help.

To compound this mistake, in April 1961 came the so-called Bay of Pigs invasion. It is almost unbelievable the number of mistakes this country made in supporting that adventure. It came about because a number of Cuban refugees and exiles from Castro's regime who had fled to the United States were able to convince this government—specifically, the Central Intelligence Agency—that the majority of the Cuban people were simply awaiting the opportune moment to oust Castro. All that was needed was a symbolic signal that their revolution would be supported. In what can only fairly be described as a fit of lunacy, the United States trained some three thousand of the exiles in guerrilla tactics, equipped them with American arms, and gave them logistic support for their "invasion." The exercise was a disaster. Within three days the entire force had been routed and most of the invaders had been taken prisoner. Possibly the only creditable action by President Kennedy throughout this disaster was his flat refusal to permit support from the U.S. Air Force, which the invaders requested and air force generals urged.

The Bay of Pigs invasion has been described as the worst miscalculation of the Cold War, and it might have been, had not Khrushchev made a worse one the following year. Judging the time ripe to improve his position vis-à-vis the revolutionary parties of South America, Khrushchev decided to arm Castro with Russian bombers, submarines, and missiles, all to be Russian-installed and Russian-manned. The missile installations were spotted in aerial photographs taken from a U-2 reconnaissance plane, and were shown to President Kennedy in the early days of October 1962.

No one realized better than the President the seriousness of the situation he faced. One mistake here, and there *would* be a war. He had, basically, three options:

1. To stall for time (American military forces were in no position to take on a world war).

2. To accept the installation of the missiles as a full-fledged military threat and to order the mobilization of the nation.

3. To find a middle course.

What Kennedy did was to find the middle course, but only after long, harried, and secret sessions with his principal advisors, after consultations with America's allies, and appeals to two peace-keeping organizations

—the Organization of American States and the United Nations. The nineteen-member OAS voted unanimous approval of the course Kennedy proposed to follow, and in the Security Council of the United Nations, the U.S. Ambassador, Adlai Stevenson, had one of his most dramatic confrontations, seen on television through much of the world, with the Soviet Ambassador, V. A. Zorin.

Stevenson, armed with the U-2 photographs, the authenticity of which Zorin denied, and demanding that United Nations observers be allowed to inspect the sites, asked ringingly:

"Do you, Ambassador Zorin, deny that the USSR has placed and is placing medium and intermediate-range missiles and sites in Cuba? Yes or no? Don't wait for the translation. Yes or no? You are in the courtroom of world opinion. You have denied they exist, and I want to know if I understood you correctly. I am prepared to wait for my answer until hell freezes over."

When Zorin still denied the existence of the missiles, Stevenson went on:

"We know the facts and so do you, sir, and we are ready to talk about them. Our job here is not to score debating points. Our job, Mr. Zorin, is to save the peace. And if you are ready to try, we are."

Kennedy's problem was that, as President of the United States and sworn to defend her against her enemies, he could not sit by and allow missiles to be installed by a foreign power less than ninety miles from his mainland; but he also wanted, if he possibly could, to avoid a full-scale confrontation with the Soviet Union.

And Kennedy's final decision was based on almost incredible amounts of information, all of it "top secret" and none of it available to a private citizen: reports on the exact "readiness" status of the army, the navy, the air force, the marines; the location of all those forces; the supplies available to them; reports from embassies around the world on the probable position of the nations in which they were located in event of war; reports from the State Department, from the Central Intelligence Agency, and every conceivable fact that could possibly help.

Consider only a few of the factors that the President had to take into consideration:

1. What would be the immediate effect of any given United States action on U.S.–Soviet relations? Would a United States do-nothing policy be regarded by Russia as a sign of weakness and would Russia then feel free to supply missile support to any Latin-American nation that wanted to implement an anti-U.S. policy? On the other hand, would a full-scale military reaction drive Russia into a position of determining that to save face with other Communist nations she must supply the missiles at any cost?

2. What effect would any United States action have on other Latin-American countries, especially those in

the Caribbean? Would they, too, regard a do-nothing
policy as a sign of weakness? Or, on the other hand,
might a strong military response lead them to believe
that the United States was determined to maintain
military control of the Western Hemisphere at any
cost?

3. What would be the effect on other countries
around the world?

Leaving aside the basic, high-level questions, there
were thousands of others, the toughest of which was:
suppose a military action started by accident? This has
happened a thousand times throughout history. Suppose President Kennedy ordered the U.S. Navy to halt
the Russian vessels carrying the missiles and, in
attempting to halt a Soviet ship, a navy destroyer fired
a shot across her bows which, instead of crossing the
bows, hit directly amidships, causing the boilers to
blow up. The Soviet ship would then sink and many
lives would be lost. Then what?

And if Kennedy had wanted to pose a full-scale
military threat, did he have the military strength to do
it? His navy, army, and air force were scattered
three-quarters of the way around the world. How
would he be able to make good on a military threat?
In international relations, there is nothing so empty as
an empty threat. Would Kennedy order the invasion
of Cuba and the removal of the missiles by force, as
both Senator Russell of Georgia and Senator Fulbright
of Arkansas advised? [1]

Kennedy's decision is now, of course, a matter of history. In his single most important and most dramatic speech, he appeared on television to explain his decision to the people of the United States, and to the world. He did not, of course, go into all the details behind the decision. The details are so complex, indeed, that entire books have been written about them, but the two most important points in Kennedy's action were his decision to impose an air-and-sea quarantine on Cuba and his announcement that any missile fired on the United States from Cuba would be considered by the United States as an attack by the Soviet Union, requiring full retaliation.

Kennedy's decision proved right. Russia's Premier Khrushchev backed down, and within a few weeks the missiles were removed.

The reason why the Kennedy handling of the Cuban crisis has been discussed in so much detail here is that it illustrates an important point about freedom of information.

It is true that the American people were not consulted at every step along the way, but that is not a question of freedom of information. Once the decision had been made, they were informed, and they were told as well how it had been arrived at.

Kennedy's decision raised a host of questions, but it must be kept in mind that similar questions could be raised about almost equally important decisions taken by five successive Presidents of the United States:

1. President Truman's decision to support France in her war against the Communist Vietminh forces.

2. President Eisenhower's decision to support the government of South Vietnam after the French defeat.

3. President Kennedy's decision to send armed, American soldiers to Vietnam to counter the military operations of the Viet Cong.

4. President Johnson's decision of almost total military support to South Vietnam, stopping short only of an actual declaration of war.

5. President Nixon's decision to end that military support.

All of these decisions had an influence on the lives of almost every American. Obviously, every citizen could not participate in the decisions; but each President knew that he was ultimately responsible to the individual citizen for his decision. Every four years citizens have the opportunity to approve or disapprove of the President's decisions through their vote. President Johnson didn't wait for the voters to decide. Knowing that his actions in the Vietnam conflict had become unpopular, he announced his decision not to run for reelection.

In his memoirs, *The Vantage Point*, Johnson told of a meeting he held in the Cabinet Room in December 1965 to discuss whether to call a halt in the bombing of North Vietnam for the second time. It had been halted seven months earlier for a short time, during which North Vietnam was able to improve its military position. Present at the meeting, among others, was Secretary of Defense Robert McNamara, Secretary of State Dean Rusk, National Security Advisor McGeorge Bundy, and Under Secretary of State George Ball.

"I asked the Secretary of State to tell me what he thought would be accomplished by a pause in the bombing," the President wrote. "His first concern, Rusk said, was American opinion. He was convinced that our people would do what had to be done in a war situation if they felt there was no alternative. We had to be able to demonstrate to them that we had done everything we could to find the way to a peaceful settlement.

" 'Haven't we done this?' I asked.

" 'To my satisfaction,' Rusk answered, 'but perhaps not to that of the American people.' "

No one will ever know whether Johnson would have fared better at the hands of public opinion had he had the almost irresistible charisma of Roosevelt, but three other factors entered into the situation that Johnson faced which were not present as Roosevelt covertly prepared for war:

1. The Vietnam War was not a war in the technical sense of the term since war can be declared only by the Congress, and this had never been done. The legal authority for the actions of five Presidents in Vietnam is based on the fact that the United States is a signatory to SEATO (South-East Asia Treaty Organi-

zation) which is designed to guarantee peace in South-East Asia and the South Pacific, and which provides for its members to consult on "other aggression." This treaty was, of course, approved by the Senate by the required two-thirds majority, as directed by the Constitution. Further, in 1964, when it was reported that American warships had been attacked in the Gulf of Tonkin, the Congress approved the so-called "Tonkin Gulf Resolution" giving the President authority to take military action in that area.

2. The Vietnam War was fought some nine thousand miles from the west coast of the United States among peoples with whom the average American had no common terms of reference in matters of cultural inheritance, tradition, language, or any of the other ties that tend to bind people of diverse nationalities.

3. No war before had ever been covered by television as was the Vietnam War. In Roosevelt's day, the war in Europe was covered by reporters from the print media, by radio broadcasters, and by newsreel cameramen. None of these had the immediacy impact of television. As the Vietnam War progressed and television devoted more and more of its coverage to it, Americans could sit in front of their television sets of an evening and see the bombs dropping and exploding, the heavy artillery guns firing, the tanks and infantry on the attack. Television brought the reality of war into the home, and pretty shocking stuff it was.

These actual scenes of the war, plus the knowledge

that it had been planned by the top officials of the United States government, headed by the President himself and, further, that the President had not taken the American people into his confidence by explaining in advance what he intended to do, gave the anti-war protests their strength.

There is no doubt that United States military involvement, from the point of view of hindsight, was a mistake of absolutely the first magnitude. In fact, it appears, again by hindsight, that the only person involved in the Vietnamese conflict who really knew what he was doing, from the time of the French defeat in 1954, was the North Vietnamese leader, Ho Chi Minh. South Vietnamese President Ngo Dinh Diem seemed to live in a dream world made up in equal parts of corruption and repression.

President Truman's decision to support the French position seems wrong; President Eisenhower's non-military reinforcement of American commitment to South Vietnam seems wrong; and so does President Kennedy's, to send in American Special Forces, the first step onto the escalator of disaster. President Johnson took the final step by ordering in United States ground forces, which eventually reached a peak of 675,000 men.

It is because of this that President Johnson's actions became the focus of freedom of information forces. Although three previous Presidents had taken, each in turn, increasingly grave steps that ultimately led to this

nation's all-but-total involvement in the war during
Mr. Johnson's years, none of their actions was sub-
jected to the withering heat of publicity focused on his.
In truth, all four Presidents, and most of their chief
advisors, were trapped in the web of history.

The American government was all too conscious of
the lessons of the Munich pact, by which, in 1938,
England and France yielded to Adolf Hitler's demand
for possession of that part of Czechoslovakia called the
Sudetenland. England's Prime Minister, Neville
Chamberlain, triumphantly proclaimed that the pact
had achieved "peace in our time," but as Hitler drove
on to new conquests, what the pact really proved was
that the only force a dictator respects is greater force.
In addition, the American government was aware of
the pattern of Communist conquest of neighboring
states, starting with the Soviet occupation of the Baltic
states of Estonia, Latvia, and Lithuania just before the
outbreak of World War II, down to the occupation of
Tibet by China in 1951.

It is not to the discredit of any of the four Presidents
cited that they did not comprehend the dissimilarity of
the situation they faced with the situation faced by
President Roosevelt and other Allied leaders during
the 1930s. Very few, if any, men have ever understood
the import of the great events in which they were
taking part until long after the events were over. And
none realized the increasing strength of the desire for
greater freedom of information.

Neil Sheehan, the chief reporter for *The New York Times* in the Pentagon Papers case, observes in the *Times* book that "knowledge of these policy debates (within the very top circles of the Johnson administration) and the dissents from the intelligence agencies might have given Congress and the public a different attitude toward the publicly announced decision of the successive administrations." So it very well might. But, even leaving apart the changing moods of the public and to a lesser extent that of the Congress, it is impossible to guess what that attitude might have been.

Mr. Sheehan wisely does not suggest any method by which knowledge of policy debates should be disseminated to the Congress or the public. The basic and very simple reason why such debates are kept secret is that it would take a very brave Cabinet officer, and one utterly heedless of his career, to make a strong case for a course of action that he knew would be highly unpopular if he thought his views were to be made public the following day.

Many people today still have clearly imprinted in their minds the havoc that the late Senator Joseph R. McCarthy wrought with the reputations of highly respected State Department officials in the 1950s by attacking them as Communists, Communist supporters, or "crypto-Communists," for opinions they had expressed years earlier, which opinions events had already proven correct. To cite but one example,

McCarthy wrecked the career of a senior and distinguished foreign service officer named John Carter Vincent because Vincent had reported, years before, that it seemed probable to him that the regime of Chiang Kai-shek was not strong enough to withstand the Communist forces in China. The fact that events had proven Vincent right made no difference to McCarthy. McCarthy also charged that General George C. Marshall and President Eisenhower were "Communist supporters," which gives a rough idea of his grip on reality.

From all this, two facts emerge clearly: it is impossible to have total freedom of information in certain areas and it is equally impossible even to define freedom of information in these same areas.

The Watergate case presents no such problems. It is without question the most damaging scandal to touch the office of the presidency since the malodorous "Teapot Dome" scandal of the Harding administration in the 1920s, and is, from the point of view of the nation's political system, far more insidious.

The story of the "Teapot Dome" case, briefly, is this: In 1909, President William Howard Taft had reserved some public lands for the use of the U.S. Navy. These lands were rich in oil deposits, and the purpose of reserving them was to insure the navy an oil supply in event of war. The most famous of these lands was Naval Petroleum Reserve No. 3, consisting of

9,500 acres of land at Teapot Dome, Natrona County, Wyoming. Secretary of the Interior Albert B. Fall was charged with conspiring to lease the oil drilling rights to a group of wealthy oil men, the most notorious of whom were Harry Sinclair, chairman of the board of the Sinclair Oil Company, who went to jail for contempt of the Senate, and Edward L. Doheny, whose Pan-American Petroleum Company later became part of the Standard Oil Company of Indiana. Doheny was found not guilty by a jury of giving a bribe of $100,000 to Fall. Fall, however, was found guilty of accepting the bribe, and went to prison. Harding's Attorney General, Harry Daugherty, barely escaped impeachment and was forced to resign. To this day, admirers of the jury system have not worked out a satisfactory explanation of how one jury could find Fall guilty of accepting a bribe from Doheny, and another jury find Doheny not guilty of having given it to him.

The insidiousness of the Watergate case arises from the use of government agencies to assist in, and later to attempt to conceal, certain felonious actions.

Dirty work at the crossroads has been a trademark of American politics virtually since the founding of the Republic; tampering with official files and using government agencies for private purposes is not exactly unknown. For example, when Robert F. Kennedy was Attorney General, he was responsible for having an agent of the Federal Bureau of Investigation question reporters in an effort to learn the sources for their stories.

But the Watergate case and its implications revealed dirty work of virtually unprecedented scope. It led, for example, to the revelation that a government agency had been involved in a break-in into the offices of a West Coast psychiatrist, Dr. Lewis J. Fielding, for the purpose of stealing his records about one of his patients, Dr. Daniel Ellsberg. Ellsberg had been an employee of the Rand Corporation, one of a handful of "think tanks" that work out for the United States government various "contingency plans" on the possible consequences of different actions by the government in a variety of highly specialized fields, including warfare. Dr. Ellsberg had been working on analyses of United States actions in Vietnam and had access to classified government papers, the so-called Pentagon Papers. The government had charged Ellsberg with taking these papers without authorization and leaking them to the press; it was presumably to discredit Ellsberg at his trial that the records of his psychiatrist were wanted.

The Watergate investigation revealed that E. Howard Hunt, Jr., one of those found guilty in the Watergate conspiracy, was able to get General Robert E. Cushman, Jr., Deputy Director of the Central Intelligence Agency, to supply him with surveillance material, a camera, a recording machine, and other materials, all of which were to be used in setting up the break-in of Dr. Fielding's office.

General Cushman's defense was that he was told that the purpose for which the material was wanted involved national security, but it hardly reflected credit either upon the agency involved or the Administration itself when it later developed that the material was for the purpose of committing an illegal burglary to obtain evidence against a private citizen against whom it is preferring charges.

The Ellsberg case was later thrown out of court because of the government's actions. Consequently, if the government had been serious in its allegations that Ellsberg had compromised national security by making the papers public, the whole point of the action was lost. But the Ellsberg break-in was only part of the Watergate case.

As has been said, Watergate has the distinction of being virtually without parallel for political shabbiness, and therein lies its insidiousness for the American political system. If it were not for this, Watergate would sound like a spy venture that might have starred the Marx brothers.

For all the elaborateness of their scheme to obtain information about the Democratic plans for the 1972 presidential campaign, the conspirators ended up with no information. Instead, they touched off a political scandal that besmirched the entire moral fabric of the

Nixon re-election campaign, and even raised serious doubts about the President's own ethical standards.

The whole Watergate break-in was marked not only by this disregard of any sort of political standards, but also by total ineptitude. Consider only the two principal operations by which the conspirators went about trying to get the information they wanted:[2]

1. A "bug" was planted in the telephone of Democratic National Committee chairman Lawrence O'Brien. It didn't work.

2. The first step the conspirators took to actually break into the Watergate building in which the Democratic headquarters were located was to tape open the automatic locks on two doors in the garage in the basement of the building during the evening of May 27. This was done so they would not have to jimmy the door open when they returned later. But an alert twenty-four-year-old security guard of the Watergate offices, named Frank Wills, making his rounds a little later, saw the tape and, thinking that it had been left accidentally by workmen, took it off. When the conspirators returned, they found the door locked. This time, they jimmied the door and re-taped the locks so that they could get out in a hurry. (It had taken half an hour to jimmy the lock.) They went upstairs to the sixth-floor offices of the Democratic committee and, while they were upstairs, Frank Wills again found the tape. This time, he called the police. The conspirators

were found in the offices, and were arrested. Information obtained? None.

As it turned out, all of the Watergate conspiracy, the use of Republican campaign funds to finance the break-in, and later to bribe the principals to take the entire blame on themselves, turned out to be unnecessary. All those involved acted as they did to ensure the re-election of President Nixon. Nixon, of course, won in a landslide, taking forty-nine of the fifty states. In fact, had the full implications of the Watergate break-in been made clear to the American people before the election, it seems inevitable that the plot would have ensured the exact opposite of its objective: the President almost certainly would have been defeated.

As it was, two of the Watergate conspirators who were convicted and sent to jail were high-level members of the Committee for the Re-Election of the President. They were G. Gordon Liddy, general counsel of the committee, and E. Howard Hunt, Jr., a former agent for the Central Intelligence Agency, who was a consultant.

Two of Nixon's former Cabinet officers were indicted by a federal grand jury on a variety of charges: his Attorney General, John N. Mitchell, and his Secretary of Commerce, Maurice H. Stans. Mr. Nixon's counsel, John W. Dean III, was intimately linked to the scandal; and one of his aides, Charles W.

Colson, was implicated in the forging of State Department cables to involve the late President John F. Kennedy in planning the assassination of the late South Vietnamese President, Ngo Dinh Diem; Mr. Nixon's acting head of the Federal Bureau of Investigation, L. Patrick Gray III, abruptly resigned. In all, a total of eighteen top government and/or high Republican party officials resigned their post, including top presidential advisors, H. R. Haldeman and John Ehrlichman.

The President, in a nationwide television speech delivered just about the time that the investigation was at its height, said that he accepted the final responsibility. The President also had said, on a number of earlier occasions, that no one on his staff was implicated.

But the President rates loyalty to himself above knowledge and experience in choosing his staff men. As a result, his staff included a preponderance of not particularly distinguished lawyers and advertising men with a very superficial understanding of the American political system, and with no sense of duty to the American people as a whole. As to any responsibility for freedom of the press, none existed.

Unlike the Teapot Dome scandal, private financial peculation was not part of the Watergate scandal, and perhaps for that very reason its threat to the political system was far greater. If the staff of any President may use the resources of the federal government to equip men for the commission of the crime of breaking and entering—as was the case in the use of CIA equipment in the Ellsberg break-in—and to falsify official State Department records—as in the case of the cables doctored to link Kennedy with Diem's assassination—all for the purpose of winning an election, then the elective process itself is being dangerously subverted.

Watergate most clearly illustrates the role of the press in your right to know, and in this connection, credit for leadership must be given to the *Washington Post*, which was subsequently awarded the Pulitzer Prize for its work in uncovering the story.

With seemingly respectable men at very nearly the highest levels of government trying to cover up the conspiracy, the average citizen would have learned very little, or nothing at all, had it not been for the investigative work done by the *Washington Post* reporters, Robert Woodward and Carl Bernstein, and a number of other reporters.

The initial investigative work was done by the reporters of only four of the 1,760 daily newspapers in the country: the *Washington Post*, the *Washington Star-News*, the *New York Times*, and the *Los Angeles Times*. George Seldes, once a newspaperman himself and author of *You Can't Print That!*, reported that the Copley, Gannett, and Newhouse papers, three of the major newspaper chains with bureaus in Washington, had no investigative reporters on the Watergate case in the months before it became headline news, and

neither did any of the three major television networks
—ABC, CBS, and NBC.[3]

The television networks are at a great disadvantage,
compared to newspapers, when it comes to doing
investigative reporting. The reason is the essence of
simplicity: money.

A newspaper has to invest in a story it wants to
explore only the salaries and expenses of the reporters
assigned, and the only equipment they need are some
notebooks and pencils.

When it comes to television coverage the costs rise
astronomically. Highly expensive equipment has to be
handled by highly paid technicians, and even the
salaries paid to television reporters who appear on
camera are substantially higher than those paid their
newspaper counterparts. For this reason, most metropolitan newspapers are able to support far larger staffs
of reporters than the television networks; they are thus
able to run down the most promising of the virtually
innumerable tips on stories that they receive every day.
Even if the tip proves worthless, as most of them do, it
is worthwhile to invest a few hours of a reporter's time
to get the one story that does pan out.

However, the *impact* of television, especially in color,
can hardly be overestimated. Actually watching an
event as it occurs brings it home to the viewer with far
more immediacy than even the most inspired reporter
can bring to a written story.

The point is made in an essay written in May 1973,

a week after the Watergate hearings had begun on television by a sixteen-year-old student in a social studies course in the Norwalk, Conn., public school system on the topic "Watergate on TV." She wrote in part:

"Now the American people will learn what happened for themselves. Televising it is better for the American people all the way around, for Americans can learn what's happening when it's happening and not wait for the newspapers (which will probably be biased). It's easier to watch than to read, too. You can learn more by watching a minute of the TV set than you can in an hour of reading. It's about time television was put to a good use, to inform the people of something that is important and deals directly with the people."

The response of the viewing public to the television coverage just about stunned the top network officials, too. While, during the first few days of coverage, the networks received several hundred complaints from viewers whose favorite daytime soap operas and quiz shows had been superseded, the complaints soon fell off, and by the time the hearings were recessed on August 7, daytime TV viewing had actually increased by 7 percent—a big jump by network standards.

The Nielsen Television Index spelled out the increase in terms of actual viewing hours: during the Watergate hearings, Nielsen found, home viewing hours for the three major networks combined were 24.4

hours daily, compared to 22.5 hours daily for enter-
tainment programs previous to Watergate. In addition
to that, the Nielsen report said, public television
stations reported an additional six hours daily viewing
time. All told, the commercial networks carried a total
of 1.6 billion hours of transmission and the public
television stations carried an additional 400 million
hours.

Between the billions of television viewing hours, and
the millions of words in the nation's newspapers and
magazines, the nation's press had certainly, in the end,
carried out its function for the American people.

3

THE NEED FOR THE
TRUTH AND
THE NEED TO BELIEVE

"I HAVE NOTHING to offer but blood, toil, tears, and sweat."

That is one of the most masterful appeals to a people on the brink of disaster ever made by a public figure. It was said by Winston Churchill to the people of Britain in May 1940, three days after he had become Prime Minister, when the nation was besieged on every front by the Nazi war machine. A few days after Churchill's speech, the British expeditionary forces were forced to flee from the small port of Dunkirk in northern France, many of them in a fleet of small, privately-owned motorboats whose owners had simply volunteered to help in the evacuation; the city of Paris was to fall to the advancing Germans and France was to capitulate; the Battle of Britain was about to begin.

In addition to its dramatic phrasing, Churchill's sentence had the all-important advantage of being the truth. It may be fairly contrasted with Hitler's statement to the German people in 1944, less than a year before the total collapse of the Third Reich: "We are succeeding in the East, and winning in the West."

The problem with perverting the truth is that it has an uncomfortable way of emerging in the end. When it does, its impact is all the more devastating for having been denied.

It is impossible to measure with any statistical yardstick the effect that the false home broadcasts had on the German people's rejection of Hitler as a national hero and Nazism as a way of government in the years after the war. But it is undeniable that the untruths had a real meaning. Admiral Karl Doenitz, who took control of the German government after Hitler committed suicide, spoke of the lethargy that had come over the German people "as a result of the paralyzing horror and immeasurable disillusionment of recent months." [1]

Franklin Roosevelt had his fair share of enemies who attempted in retrospect to equate his promise not to send American soldiers abroad with the palpable lies of the Nazi propaganda machine, but the analogy does not bear examination.

When Hitler made his statement, it was a flat contradiction of the facts as they then existed. When

Roosevelt made his statement, he may have been
laboring under an illusion that he would not have to
supply troops to Europe, but he certainly was not
subverting the truth, and the illusion was not his alone.
It should not be forgotten that until only a few months
before France fell, the French forces looked stronger—
on paper—than the Germans. France had mobilized
110 divisions, compared to less than 100 for Germany;
more than that, Germany had committed the bulk of
her army to the Eastern front, following the invasion of
Poland.[2] Churchill had described the French Army as
"the most perfectly trained" in Europe.[3]

So it is hardly surprising that Roosevelt, as Robert
E. Sherwood wrote in *Roosevelt and Hopkins*, until the
fall of France, "was wishfully hoping that Britain and
France would prove indomitable in the West, that the
Soviet Union would keep Germany contained in the
East . . ."

This illustration has been gone into at such length
because the entire concept of freedom of information
must be based on trust, which in turn can be constructed only on a foundation of truth.

During the preparation of this book, hundreds of
conversations were held with young people to get their
reactions to various questions. The conversations were
confined entirely to news, and to news about political,
social, and economic developments. No question of
trust arises if a five-alarm fire is reported in a

newspaper, nor if it is reported that the New York
Giants football team beat the Green Bay Packers by a
score of 21 to 17.

If, however, a President reports that he is taking
such-and-such an action for such-and-such a reason or,
to carry it one step further, if a newspaper or television
reporter says that the President will do such-and-such,
then the question of trust does arise.

And that was the common denominator found
running through those hundreds of conversations: the
need for trust.

To cite a specific example, consider again for a
moment President Kennedy's action in the Cuban
missile crisis. The President announced his action, and
explained at some length that it was based on the
premise that the missiles represented a direct military
threat to the United States; further, that since they
were being installed by Russian technicians and were
to be manned by Russian experts, they would no more
be under Cuban control than the warships of the U.S.
Navy in Guantanamo Bay were under control of the
Cubans.

In the conversations with young people, this topic
was always brought up, and the question posed: "Was
President Kennedy's a proper action?"

The answer was virtually unanimously, yes.

"On what do you base your conclusion?"

And the answer, again virtually always: "We trusted
President Kennedy."

Again and again, in fact, no matter what the topic under discussion, toward the end one of the young people was almost sure to say: "Well, what it comes down to is that you have to trust someone."

There also emerged, tacitly, a factor that applies equally to adults: people *want* to trust the President.

This statement may seem to be contradicted by the number of anti-politics books that have appeared within the last ten years (Professor John H. Bunzel's *Anti-Politics in America* is one of the best of the most recent ones) that deal with what is seemingly a totally different American attitude: that Americans, far from *wanting* to trust a political figure of whatever stature, actually pride themselves on distrusting *all* politicians.

There are two factors in American society to explain this. The first is that even through the Constitutional Convention in 1787, Americans were determined not to fall into the trap of respecting party labels—Tories, Whigs, and so on—which they felt had helped make England a class society. The second is the emergence of the American pioneer.

By all odds this contributed most to the American distrust of the politician. By the simple fact of being a pioneer, a landholder, and a man of property, the individual American had become a person of significance, which he could never have hoped to become in the nation from which he had emigrated. And what had the politician done to assist him in achieving this status? Within a period of less than three generations

the property-holding qualification for voting was elim-
inated. But this new emancipation also brought with it
a populist contempt for the intellectuals who had
forged the Revolution and planned the future of the
country.

Only two years after John Adams and Thomas
Jefferson died, on July 4, 1826, the supporters of
Andrew Jackson were shouting, during his 1828 cam-
paign for the presidency:

> *He's none of your New England stock,*
> *Or your gentry-proud Virginians,*
> *But a regular western fighting cock*
> *With Tennessee opinions.*[4]

Clinton Rossiter, in his *Parties and Politics in America*,
defined this as "the strong antipolitical bias that crops
up in our folklore."

Despite all of this, the need to believe remains and is
stronger today than ever before.

On January 17, 1974, for example, *The New York
Times* reported on the problems congressmen found
during tours of their districts during the congressional
recess. The headline said: "Greatest Domestic Problem—What to Believe."

The list of disbeliefs was long, from the reality of the
energy crisis to the validity of the Watergate tapes. It is
important to note, however, in discussing freedom of
information, that these elements of disbelief were, and
are, subjects of public discussion.

Because of these open channels of information it seems patently impossible for the United States to experience such sudden wrenches of public images as the de-Stalinization program launched by Khrushchev, which required the rewriting of Russian history books and encyclopedias to prove that Stalin, far from being the kindly father of the Russian people as he had previously been depicted, was actually an assassin, a mass-murderer, and a betrayer of the people's hopes. The evidence also lies in the public debate, in newspapers, over the works of such renowned contemporary Russian writers as Alexander Solzhenitsyn (*One Day in the Life of Ivan Denisovich* and *The First Circle*), and in smaller matters like the quality of the nylon stockings and cotton floor mops on sale in state-operated stores that undoubtedly impinge more deeply upon the lives of individual Russians than the ideological struggles over great reputations.

Shortly after World War II, for example, the Russians found it necessary to transfer thousands of their occupation troops from East Germany to the uttermost eastern provinces of Russia because the troops, according to the Russians, were becoming corrupted by the effete bourgeois way of life in East Germany. Even considering the depths to which the ravages of war and defeat had lowered the East German standard of living, the Russian soldiers were so impressed by what Westerners take for granted—individual homes, and apartments in which no more than two people had to share a room, modern plumbing, privately-owned shops and automobiles— that the Russian government thought it wise to get the soldiers away from temptation.

And, more recently, the visit of Soviet Premier Leonid Brezhnev to the United States made clear further difficulties for a controlled press. A dispatch from Moscow to the *New York Times* reported that it was not easy for *Pravda* to explain a number of seemingly contradictory facts:

1. If capitalistic big business in the United States is so oppressive of workers' rights in its own country and so opposed to the success of socialist republics abroad, why was it that American business was so eager to welcome Brezhnev to the United States, and to open trade negotiations?

2. And, on the other hand, if the American trade union movement is so spiritually allied with the aspirations of trade union movements in socialist countries, why was it so opposed to these enlargements of trade agreements?

3. If the United States is so racist a nation, still holding the black man in the yoke of oppression, how had the nation's third largest city—Los Angeles— managed only a short while earlier to elect a black man its mayor?

There is no indication, certainly at the present time, that the mass of the Soviet people are concerned about inconsistencies in the Soviet reporting of news from the

United States, any more than Americans would be concerned about similar inconsistencies in reporting about the Soviet Union in the American press. Beyond the geographical remoteness of the United States from Russia, the Russian people have for generations been accustomed, virtually from infancy onward, to suspect everything western. The Czars for centuries were almost pathologically afraid of western ideas, and this paranoia was wholeheartedly fostered by the Soviets, who similarly wanted no popular questioning of their infallibility. If you are taught from the cradle on, through every resource of information, even including kindergarten textbooks, that the western nations are evil, oppressive, and the deadly enemy of your country, it is hardly likely that a few contradictions in the image given you of life in the United States will in any way shake your convictions.

In the western democracies, however, the people have been accustomed to a news flow that, by and large, reflects the truth.

The qualification "by and large" is necessary because in war, as the old adage has it, anything goes. To have suggested, in the United States in 1942, that while their leaders had embarked them on a plan for the conquest of the entire Far East, the Japanese people as a whole shared certain basic qualities of humanity with the Americans, would have been asking for a tar-and-feathering at the hands of the mob. Even the internment of nearly one million American citizens

of Japanese descent in detention camps along the West
Coast—a more flagrant violation of civil rights than
President Lincoln's suspension of the Bill of Rights
provisions during the Civil War—was not protested by
even the most ardent defenders of civil rights.

But, war apart, Americans are accustomed to demanding, and generally getting, news as close to the
truth as possible. And as much of the truth as possible.
While, as has previously been shown, people are
perfectly willing to know that part of the truth is being
withheld from them on the grounds of national
security, the trust that is implicit in this is destroyed if
it later develops that national security was, in fact, not
involved.

A constant difficulty is that the question of national
security cannot be precisely defined. It is here that so
often, all through the modern history of the relations
between the press and the government, the charges
and the countercharges fly.

What may seem to a government official to be
clearly a matter of national security may, to a reporter,
seem an attempt by that official to conceal public
information.

On balance, it seems to serve the individual citizen
better to have this constant conflict continue rather
than attempt to control it. After all, by their very
framing of the words of the Constitution, the Founding
Fathers showed clearly that they understood that men
will always be jealous of their own powers and their

own prerogatives, and they wisely refrained from laying down hard and fast laws to try to cover every possible contingency.

It is precisely for this reason that the conflict among the three official arms of government—the executive, the legislative, and the judicial—exists today, has always existed, and always will. Due to the absolutely unpredictable equation of human behavior, each arm of the government will forever be complaining that the others are infringing upon its prerogatives, and will forever be right. That is why the pre-eminent unofficial arm of government—the press—will also forever be at war with the three official arms.

In considering the role of the press, however, a totally different factor must be taken into consideration: that the press is itself a private, money-making, business. (The term "press" here, it should again be emphasized, in this generic sense also includes television.) However much the press may speak or write of its responsibilities to its readers—and, by and large, responsible press representatives today take these responsibilities very seriously—the press also has a responsibility to a different master, the owners. And the owners, in turn, are very well aware of the fact that their continued operation depends on their greatest source of revenue, their advertisers.

It is not at all surprising today—despite the news media's very large contribution to the public understanding of public affairs—that the crusade for consumers' rights should have been spearheaded by an unheard-of lawyer named Ralph Nader, who first came to public notice in 1965 with the publication of his book *Unsafe at Any Speed.*

It is quite probable that there were at least a thousand reporters on various newspapers across the country who knew as much about the weaknesses and flaws of American automobiles as Nader did and who could have, within a few weeks or months, turned out as comprehensive a survey of them as he did, but newspapers and other media depend very heavily on automobile advertisements to stay in business. Nader's publisher, Grossman, did not.

There is, then, another danger to the freedom of information—the economic dependence on advertising for revenue.

In the eternal battle between the press and the government, it is true there are plenty of men in government who would very much like the press to be not exactly muzzled, but certainly have considerably less freedom than it now enjoys to speak its mind.

But, on the other hand, it must also be remembered that when the press stands upon its Constitutional guarantees as a special institution in its demands for total freedom, it is taking somewhat the position of the owners of major league baseball clubs who on the one hand demand special considerations from Congress and the courts on the ground that baseball is "an American institution and the national sport," yet who run their franchises with a contempt for the feelings of their customers that would put General Motors out of business in a month.

When Jefferson wrote such trenchant lines as "Where the press is free and every man able to read, all is safe," [5] he was writing in the same eighteenth-century frame of mind that saw democracy as the end to the sufferings of man. Jefferson's feelings were molded by dealing with a press that was, in fact, free not only from governmental interference but also largely from economic forces. The eighteenth-century editor or publisher needed only a very modest capital to rent or buy a printing press and other supplies, plus the brains to have something cogent to write and the literacy to make it understood.

Contrast that with today. No one has seriously considered starting a new newspaper in New York City for twenty-odd years now; it is estimated that it would cost somewhere between $25 and $30 million to start a paper and at least $1 million a month to keep it in operation for a year. On a lesser scale, this is true throughout the United States, down to all but the smallest communities.

Many studies have been made of the reasons for the changing status of the press since Jefferson's day, but the principal one is that the rationale of the press has become that of profit. It has been increasingly profitable to the owners of communications media to have as many monopolies as possible.

The most recent survey by *Editor & Publisher*, the trade magazine of the newspaper industry, taken in 1972, shows that only three cities in the United States have competing morning papers (New York, Boston, Chicago) and only six competing evening papers (Chicago, Washington, Baltimore, Philadelphia, Fort Worth, San Antonio). In twenty years, it is predicted, *all* United States newspapers will be owned by chains.

New York City is the most dramatic example. Fifty years ago, the city supported fourteen daily newspapers, seven in the morning—the *American, Herald, News, Sun, Times, Tribune,* and *World*—and seven in the evening—the *Evening Sun, Evening World, Globe, Journal, Mail, Post,* and *Telegram.* Only fifteen years ago, the number of papers had been reduced to a total of seven—the *Herald Tribune, Mirror, News,* and *Times* in the morning, and the *Journal-American, Post,* and *World-Telegram & Sun* in the afternoon. (The very names show the amalgamation of ownerships.) Today there are only three, the *Times* and *News* in the morning and the *Post* in the afternoon. There is, in addition, the *Wall Street Journal,* but this is what is known as a "specialized circulation" newspaper.

As far as freedom of information is concerned, such a reduction in the number of newspapers—and the same is true in all cities where competitive ownership is replaced by monopoly—is reflected not only in the reduction of differing points of view on news development, but also in the amount of news reported.

It is very easy to make this clear. Every newspaper, and every other medium of communication, appeals first to what it regards as the common interests of its audience. Everyone, for example, is presumed to be interested in the weather, so almost all media feature weather reports; all persons are presumed to be interested in birth and death, so even the news magazines have sections devoted to those topics, and so on with national news, international news, local news, sports, feature stories, special departments devoted to fashions, household hints, comic strips, and crossword puzzles. Every newspaper also recognizes that it has sizable blocks of specialized readerships, which it caters to in almost exact proportion to the number of readers in that category. For example, a newspaper with a large Polish audience will set aside a certain amount of space for Polish-American news; a newspaper with a sizable readership among older people will have a senior citizens section; newspapers will have columns on fishing news, pet care, home repair, coin collecting—whatever they believe will increase their readership.

This criterion applies also to news coverage, and that is the area in which the benefit of competition is most obvious to the reader. When two newspapers are competing for readers, the news is more completely covered and more news is covered; when one paper achieves a monopoly, it is all too easy to cut costs by cutting down on specialized news stories and on the

quality of the coverage of those stories that are
covered. When the *Herald Tribune* was still competing
with the *Times* in New York, for example, it was ritual
for the editorial staffs of each paper to get the first
copies of the other to come off the presses in early
evening to see if they had missed any important stories
and, if they had, to cover the lapse as quickly as
possible in the next edition. With the demise of the
Tribune, this sense of urgency no longer pervades the
Times. The *Times,* not entirely correctly, does not
regard the *News* as competition since the *News* is a
tabloid and relies heavily on dramatic news pictures
for its appeal.

There are exceptions to this general rule; there are
hard-working and conscientious editors and editorial
staffs on monopoly newspapers, but for the most part
they are exceptions.

It is not simply on individual newspapers or in
monopoly radio or television stations that this danger
to freedom of information exists. For in all chain
operations, the quality of the product tends to be the
same. Just as the frozen foods offered for sale in a
supermarket chain store in Baltimore are likely to be
similar to the frozen foods offered by a store in the
same chain in San Diego, so the editorial approach
offered by two newspapers, or radio or television
stations, belonging to the same chain in two widely
separated cities—say, Bangor, Maine, and Phoenix,
Arizona—are likely to be the same. Not that the

editorial *topic* would be the same, but if the chain owner's philosophy were highly conservative, the editorial *approach* would be the same in the two cities, and similarly if he were liberal.

Now, to the reader of these monopoly papers, what does this do to the concept of truth? The truth is generally arrived at, in day-to-day life, only by listening to or reading the views of men of probity who hold widely differing views, and it is here that the monopoly press, no matter how high the principles of the individual editors or publishers, fails the public. For the monopoly press never basically presents more than one point of view.

4

THE RESPONSIBILITY
AND IRRESPONSIBILITY
OF THE PRESS

IN THE HERITAGE of the press there are two genes
forever at odds, continually struggling between themselves for dominance. One of them is the noble
tradition of informing the public as fully and truthfully
as possible, fighting the good fight. The other comes
down to the basic matter of money.

Executives of the press, especially the chief corporate
executives, spend a good deal of time and space
reminding the public of their sense of dedication to
their honorable tradition, but at the same time these
executives know that they are first responsible to their
own financial offices for their profit-and-loss statements. And, all too often, they are less responsive than
most money-making corporations to their public responsibility.

If, for example, the General Motors Corporation turns out a shoddy and ill-made car, it stands a good chance of being forced to recall it, or of being certain to lose a customer for life. If a publisher turns out a shoddy and ill-made newspaper, on the other hand, there is no recourse against it, especially in a monopoly city. What is the reader to do? To whom is he going to complain? What if he does decide to boycott the paper for life? General Motors doesn't really like to lose even one customer, because its revenue depends directly on the consumer; the newspaper publisher, television station, or network owner doesn't depend for revenue on the individual consumer; he depends on the advertiser. Of course, he'll eventually lose his advertiser unless his product sells, but the loss of the sale of an automobile is greater than that of a newspaper.

The only alternative to the advertiser is, of course, the government. The essential weakness of the government press has been discussed too often to need repetition. As for the weaknesses of the press in a democracy, it may be useful to recall Winston Churchill's comment about democracy—that it is perhaps the most inefficient form of government ever devised, but that he could think of none better.

While it is true that there are far too many individual organs of the press that are irresponsible when it comes to reporting the truth, there are, on the other hand, so many countervailing forces today that eventually the truth does emerge.

The central weakness in the western system of democratic journalism is that there is no impartial arbiter of truthful responsibility, except in the most egregious cases of libel. And even in many of those cases, it must be proven that an untrue story was published with intent to cause harm.

The majority of charges against the irresponsibility of the press come from public figures, who occupy a special position, since the libel laws do not protect them. A minority of the press exists on the publication of scandal stories, feeding principally off the lives of prominent persons, basically secure in the knowledge that they will not be prosecuted in court because of the principal's feeling that it's not really worth the trouble. Every person in the public eye knows the sort of story in that kind of publication: "*Is* Politician X the real father of actress Y's child?"

Or the story might speculate about the possible physical deficiencies of public figures. It would be impossible to calculate the number of published stories about the physical ailments of recent Presidents that might, if true, have proven them incompetent to govern. The more scurrilous of them were so libelous as to be unrepeatable. Of the non-libelous stories, James MacGregor Burns, in his book *John Kennedy, a Political Profile*, points out the problems that Kennedy had in trying to quell the rumors, following his back operation in 1954, that he had incurable cancer, tuberculosis, or some other serious malady, and the rumors, in 1959, that he had Addison's disease, a frequently fatal infection of the adrenal glands. (Incidentally, the stories continued, despite Kennedy's efforts.)

The problems facing the responsible editors in handling stories such as the one about Kennedy and Addison's disease are not easy ones to solve, and are further complicated by the fact that the medical authorities themselves hedged the question of whether the President actually had a mild case of the disease, or whether some other condition was causing the malfunctioning of the glands.[1]

There are, however, clear-cut cases in which the irresponsibility of the "responsible" press is patent; cases in which the press, despite its consistent demand for scrupulous observation of its own rights, does not hesitate to trample on the rights of others in its all-out competition in covering a major news story.

The most dramatic recent example, as reported by the President's Commission on the Assassination of President John F. Kennedy, was the performance of the press that led to the assassination of Lee Harvey Oswald, the President's accused murderer, within the headquarters of the Dallas police itself. The commission found that the insatiable demands of the press for total coverage of every detail of Oswald's handling by the police helped precipitate the final events that led to Oswald's death. The President's commission contented itself with suggesting that the press establish a code of professional responsibility, which later was given the approval of the American Society of Newspaper Editors. The action of the editors is unfortunately somewhat like the owners of the National Football Conference agreeing that professional football is getting pretty rough and that someone really ought to do something about it sometime.

To the credit of newspapers generally, however, there is considerable evidence that they have, within the past generation, become more responsible than they were in the days of so-called yellow journalism. This may be due in part to the changing texture of American life as a whole.

During the first third of this century newspapers were, to all intents and purposes, the sole source of news; there was, of course, no television, and radio did not come into its own as a medium until the 1930s. In the metropolitan centers of the country, a substantial portion of newspaper circulation came from street sales—newspapers that were bought at newsstands or from newsboys who hawked them in the streets. Today, that sort of newsboy has all but disappeared from the streets of our major cities, and newsstands themselves are slowly but steadily disappearing as well.

This method of selling newspapers, however, is important to note because it led to two things: the use of large-type headlines or "scare heads," to attract purchasers; and emphasis on the more sensational aspects of news stories for the same reason.

This sort of journalism dominated the newspaper

world of the United States all through the second half of the nineteenth century. Even the picture journalism familiar to today's readers in such newspapers as the *New York Daily News* and a variety of picture magazines was foreshadowed by the lavish use of black-and-white illustrations of the artist's version of what had happened in such great events as the sinking of the battleship *Maine.* The fact that the artist's version later turned out to be at considerable variance with the facts made little difference.

By the time of the Spanish-American War, yellow journalism played so important a role that a number of historians have argued that, without the press, there would have been no war at all. This was the era when the two titans of yellow journalism, Joseph Pulitzer and William Randolph Hearst, were already locked in combat for domination of the news market, and the publishers and editors of what later became quite "respectable" papers, notably James Gordon Bennett of the *New York Herald* and Charles A. Dana of *The Sun*, were only too willing to join in the struggle.

Now, innuendoes about politicians may be regarded as relatively unimportant distortions, or fabrications, of the news. But when the same technique is applied to public affairs which have or could have a serious effect on the lives of the readers of these newspapers, it becomes a totally different matter.

An interesting parallel may be drawn between the conduct of the press in the Spanish-American War and

in the Vietnam conflict. The press was far more
intimately involved with the causes, start, and conduct
of the Spanish-American War than the Vietnam War.
In 1898, among the major American papers, only the
Louisville Courier-Journal and the *New York Post* suggested
that perhaps, whatever the merits of the cause of the
Cuban revolutionists against the rule of Spain, the
United States was not justified in going to war with
Spain over the problem. But the other newspapers
almost unanimously supported the war just as, toward
the end, the majority of the newspapers of the 1970s
opposed the American involvement in Vietnam.

The Spanish-American War also may have marked
the end of the romantic figure of the great war
correspondent as an important factor in public information, though the image has lasted in fiction, even
until today.

Through all the years that Hearst was in active
control of his newspapers, he spared no expense in
hiring the best talent available. The American Newspaper Guild found the Hearst papers the most difficult
of all to organize in the 1930s because Hearst paid his
reporters salaries well in excess of those paid on other
papers, and far in excess of those proposed by the
Guild, though he was as adamantly anti-union as the
other major publishers.[2]

Hearst also believed in "saturating" major stories by
sending scores of reporters to cover them. At least fifty
reporters wrote about the Spanish-American War for

Hearst, and twenty artists did nothing except illustrate it. These reporters and illustrators were not mere nobodies, either. One example of Hearst's more famous correspondents was Richard Harding Davis, then so well known that when he and Theodore Roosevelt, commander of the Rough Riders, met, the newspaper account stated that Colonel Roosevelt was introduced to the famous war correspondent Richard Harding Davis.[3] Another example was Stephen Crane, author of *The Red Badge of Courage*. Hearst's illustrators included the most famous of all the artists of the American Old West, Frederic Remington.

But, as Davis himself later wrote, the day of the "great" correspondent began to decline after the Spanish-American War.[4] Davis ascribed the decline to the rise of technology—the telegraph and the cable. Until that time, even the most important of news dispatches had been handwritten and sent by mail. The reporter took pride in the quality of his writing, and his audience found satisfaction in reading them. Dispatches of five to ten thousand words, printed in their entirety, were by no means a novelty. During the Spanish-American War, however, this began to change. This was probably not due only, as Davis thought, to more reliance on the telegraph and cable, but also to the demand for quickness and brevity in dispatches as the number of newspapers and magazines increased during the opening decade of the twentieth century.

For a variety of reasons, the day of the leisurely reader was declining, and it may have been this as much as the increasing reliance on telegraph that began to diminish the importance of the once-glamorous by-line correspondent. Lincoln Steffens thought that the decline was due to the fact that publishers were beginning to look on their papers more and more as profit-making and power-creating enterprises first, and as responsible editorial voices second. Hearst and Pulitzer, for example, although they frequently wrote of the need for editorial integrity, when it came to the circulation wars, were far more interested in stories that would sell newspapers than in the more sober approach to responsible reporting that Adolph Ochs was insisting on in *The New York Times*. Hearst and Pulitzer wanted power and wanted riches; the way to achieve them then, in the newspaper publishing business, was to get circulation, and the way to do that was to get big-name reporters, sensational stories, ever-bigger headlines, and stunningly dramatic illustrations.[5]

It is interesting to consider that, in a sense, television, the most sophisticated news transmission we know today, has adopted part of that approach. For today, as readers three-quarters of a century ago bought newspapers to read stories under the by-lines of such world-famous names as Richard Harding Davis and Stephen Crane, and the newspapers strove to enhance the fame of their writers, so nowadays do television viewers tune in to see the news as reported by a Walter Cronkite or a John Chancellor, and the television networks work to establish and nurture the importance of such men.

There is an important difference between then and now, however. It is impossible to imagine today, for example, the editor of a television network, or of a newspaper, sending a cable similar to the one William Randolph Hearst sent to the famous American artist Frederic Remington, whom he had commissioned to supply illustrations for the Cuban war. Remington, shortly after his arrival on the scene, had cabled Hearst: "Everything is quiet. There is no trouble. There will be no war. I wish to return."

To which Hearst cabled back: "Please remain. You furnish the pictures and I'll furnish the war." [6]

The problem that this sort of attitude, on the part of publisher, editor, or reporter, poses for the reader must be obvious.

If the man responsible for presenting the news to the readers is absolutely convinced of the rightness of his cause, the stories that appear are not so much designed to supply information upon which individual judgments may be made, as to create or re-enforce biases.

The editor of a paper that has a basically conservative readership, built over the years by its own handling of the news, tends to edit news in a way tailored to the interests of the readership that it has built.

To make this specific: suppose a new model city were being built along the lines of the model cities already built and being built in many nations, including the United States. And suppose that you were given the power and the means to establish a newspaper that would best serve this new community.

Your basic concept of the newspaper relies on the very word "news." First, you would want to provide the community with all the news about all events that could have an effect on its life, as well written as possible.

That means that you would report, correctly and faithfully, such matters as municipal action on power supply, street repair, sewage systems, and so on; your own opinion on the merits or defects of those municipal programs would presumably be confined to your editorial page.

Suppose, as the paper's publisher, you were absolutely convinced that enlargement of the power supply system, for example, would be a serious error. From a moral point of view, you might have a "good" or a "bad" reason for this. Today, the "good" reason might be that opposition to this extension of the power system would help contribute to man's preservation of his own environment. Limited natural resources would be threatened, fish and bird life destroyed, and so on. The "bad" reason today might be that you were supporting the already swollen profits of the utility suppliers.

But, only slightly more than a generation ago, when

the Tennessee Valley Authority was being established, the arguments would have been reversed. Then the "good" reason would be that electric power was being brought to a community sorely in need of it; the "bad" reason would be that you were more concerned with the environment than with the welfare of the people who would be served.

As the responsible publisher of this newspaper, you confine your editorial opinion to your editorial columns. You report in your news columns that such-and-such is happening on the power issue; on your editorial page you voice your judgment as to whether this is "good" or "bad." No human problem can be discussed in purely theoretical terms, however, and this clear separation of the powers of the press almost never exists.

Start with the reporter, the first interpreter of the news. Now, even a reporter determined to be as absolutely impartial as he can be, reporting the position of both sides without prejudice toward either, has his work cut out for him, because he must use his own judgment as to what is newsworthy.

The problem arises, for the reader, when the reporter is already convinced that one side or the other is correct.

In a totalitarian state, the reader knows that the reporter—and the paper—is dedicated to the cause of the state.

The difficulty for a reader in a democratic state is

that he assumes that the reporter and the paper are striving at least to report the facts fairly, and that the opinions of the editor or publisher will appear on the editorial page. If that is not true, then the reader is not so much being denied information as he is being given biased information that can hardly provide the basis for a reasonable judgment of his own.

This is by no means so flagrant a malfeasance against the rights of the reader as those cited earlier, nor is it nearly so widespread in the press of the nation, but it does exist.

5

SANCTITY OF THE SOURCE

THE PROBLEMS FOR freedom of information as posed by government-press relationship are of a different nature and fall into two categories: first, the attempt of the government to force reporters, newspapers, and even television networks to reveal to the government news and the sources of news that the press has gathered; second, the problems of the press in getting public information from the government.

The attempt to prevent the reporter from protecting his sources is nothing new. Indeed, this press-government struggle may be traced as far back as Peter Zenger, who (as discussed in Chapter 1) refused to disclose the names of contributors to his *New York Weekly Journal.* The first major modern case to come to public attention was that of James Simonton, a Washington reporter for the original *New York Times,* founded in 1851 by three men, the best known of whom was Henry J. Ramond, a politician and newspaperman. Simonton had written that a number of congressmen were getting as much as $1,500 for their votes on measures before Congress.[1] Simonton refused to name the persons who had given him his information and was held in the custody of the sergeant-at-arms for nineteen days; he was then released for the very simple reason that he told Congress that he would never reveal the names of his informants no matter how long he was held.

But the dispute over the rights to protect sources has never been more heated than it is today.

On the one hand is the reporter's persuasive claim that if he cannot protect his sources, no one will trust him enough to give him the information necessary to do effective reporting.

Three specific cases formed the basis for a 1972 decision by the Supreme Court on this very complicated problem. Two of them concern confidential information given to newsmen by the Black Panther organization. These were:

1. The case of Paul Pappas, a reporter-cameraman for television station WTEV-TV in New Bedford, Massachusetts. In the midst of racial disorders in New Bedford in 1970, Pappas was allowed into the Black Panther headquarters on his promise that what he saw would be held strictly in confidence. A few months later, however, Pappas was summoned before a Bristol

County (Mass.) grand jury and was questioned about all aspects of his coverage of the story, including what happened inside the Black Panther headquarters and the names of the persons there. Pappas answered all questions except the ones he had promised not to answer.

2. The case of Earl Caldwell, a reporter for *The New York Times* assigned to the paper's San Francisco bureau, who had written a number of stories for the *Times* about the Black Panthers in California. Early in 1970, Caldwell was subpoenaed to appear before a federal grand jury in San Francisco, but Caldwell and the *Times* fought the case all the way to the Supreme Court.

3. The case—not involving the Black Panthers—of Paul M. Branzburg, a reporter for the *Louisville Courier-Journal* who wrote a series of articles for that paper late in 1969 on the use, sale, and manufacture of drugs by youthful "hippies" in Louisville. Branzburg, like Pappas and Caldwell, got his information by promising anonymity to the people he interviewed; and the authorities followed the same procedure as in the other two cases: Branzburg was called before a grand jury, refused to answer questions on the identity of the people to whom he had given fictitious names in his stories, and the case was appealed up to the highest court.

On June 29, 1972, the Supreme Court ruled, by a

decision of five-to-four, that reporters do *not* have the right to withhold confidential information from grand juries.

The decision had repercussions in two areas. The first, of course, impinges directly upon freedom of information.

It is true that "the anonymous informant" story in newspapers has inherent dangers of its own. If there were no check on the publication of anonymous information it would be perfectly possible for a politician or a venal reporter, or both in combination, to publish a scurrilous story and then seek the refuge of anonymity. This is by no means an imaginary danger, but it happens infrequently enough in major newspapers so that it can hardly be regarded as a threat to freedom of information, and it hardly outweighs the damage done to the drying-up of sources of information to honorable reporters. Caldwell himself wrote that after the court decision no outside reporter could be expected to be allowed entree to Black Panther headquarters. It may be assumed that the Black Panthers would have allowed no one, including Caldwell, to see anything they really wanted to keep secret, but that may be beside the point. The point is that outside reporters would not be allowed in and that source of information would be lost.

The second repercussion that the Supreme Court decision had has less relevance to freedom of information, and that was the discussion, principally in legal circles, on the function of the grand jury.

The grand jury system, which is provided for in the Fifth Amendment, is descended from the English Common Law code that stretches back to the Middle Ages and that was designed, in essence, to protect the middle and lower classes against the excesses of the upper. To make sure that an individual could not be brought to trial on arbitrary charges, English law and the Fifth Amendment require that, to quote the Fifth Amendment, "No person shall be held to answer for a capital, or otherwise infamous crime, unless on a presentment or indictment of a Grand Jury . . ."

In other words—and it was this part of the Supreme Court decision that so many responsible legal authorities criticized—a grand jury cannot be used as a "fishing expedition." The basic function of the grand jury is to make a decision on whether the evidence against a specific individual concerning a specific crime is enough to indict him, and it is for this reason that witnesses are subpoenaed. A grand jury is not convened for the purpose of deciding who is guilty of the crime or even, as in some extreme cases, of who *might* be guilty of a crime that has not taken place.

For example, assuming that the prosecuting attorney proposes to ask an indictment against John Doe for the murder of Samuel Roe, a proper question for him to ask a grand jury witness is:

"Did you see John Doe with a smoking .38-calibre revolver in his hand standing only four feet from the body of Samuel Roe, who had just been shot with a .38-calibre revolver?"

On the basis of the answer to that question the grand jury may decide that John Doe should be indicted for murder.

But suppose the prosecuting attorney knows only that Samuel Roe has been shot, and that John Doe belongs to an organization that has sworn to kill Mr. Roe. Suppose further that the organization to which Mr. Doe belongs had admitted a reporter, under pledge of secrecy, to the headquarters of the group.

Under terms of the Fifth Amendment, the prosecuting attorney could call the reporter in and ask him the same questions he would ask any possible witness who might give him the information necessary to secure an indictment.

What the prosecuting attorney may *not* ask is the one basic question that the three reporters refused to answer: "Do you know anybody who might have done this?"

In other words, according to any known interpretation of Common Law or of the Fifth Amendment, no grand jury may be convened for the purpose of asking those called before it whether it is possible that there *might* be evidence that could form the basis for an indictment.

Whatever the legal repercussions of the test cases

brought before the Supreme Court, and its decisions on them, there seems little doubt that they have made the role of the press in investigative stories much more difficult, for in the past one of the assets that the press had was its channel to non-authoritative sources. After all, the judicial branch of the government, reaching down even to local attorneys general, is presumed to have access to all official sources of information within their jurisdiction, whether it uses them or not.

It is by going outside these sources that the press has played its important role. If, let us say, a mayor is diverting public funds into his own pocket, his actions are presumably not known in official channels. If they are, there is the even more serious problem of general official corruption. An unofficial source, however, may have knowledge of this peculation and may, for one reason or another, be averse to taking legal action. It is through the finding of these unofficial sources that the press has been able to play its role.

Yet even the Supreme Court decision does not seem to be the final word: there are bills pending in Congress and in various state capitols that would give varying degrees of immunity to reporters, much in the same way that priests are under compulsion not to reveal what members of their flock confess to them, and lawyers not to reveal confidential relationships with their clients.

The problem with all of these proposed laws, however, is that no one seems to be able to agree on the terms, including newsmen and newsmen's organizations.

The second problem concerning government–press relations, that of the press obtaining information from government sources, has existed ever since the Civil War.

This phase does not concern those kinds of information, touched on briefly earlier, generally understood to be properly classified as government secrets such as information on military operations under way, information on high-level diplomatic negotiations under way, and, since the 1940s, information on nuclear fission projects.

It may be useful to remember that, though civilian agencies now use military classifications for information, such as "Secret," the classification of military information stretches far back into the dim mists of ancient history when warfare began to take on something of the shape it maintained through World War II. For centuries, one accepted method of getting military information about the enemy was through torture of captured prisoners, but eventually opposing commanders saw that it was futile to torture men who didn't have any information. Probably the very first of the early conquerors, therefore, developed the concept of what today's military calls the "right to know." By this, subordinate commanders are told only what they need to know, what they have the right to know in order to carry out successfully the operations assigned to them. In fact, a shrewd subordinate would quickly see that it was to his own benefit not to know any more than he positively had to. This concept, still in force, is fostered not so much by the fear of torture—although that seems to be coming back into fashion in armies around the world today after centuries of effort to have it officially outlawed—as by the fear of being accused of leaking information. If there is a "leak," and you didn't have the information in the first place, you can hardly be charged with being the guilty party.

Today, at the very top level of government classification comes the stamp "Eyes Only" for a top official, such as the President; general classifications after that in descending order of importance are "Top Secret," "Secret," "Confidential," and "Restricted."

The authority for classification comes from the top down. In other words, a President is presumably the only executive who can decide what materials are so important that they may be classified "Eyes Only," and who has the authority to make the "Eyes Only" classification for him. While final responsibility for the decision rests upon the President, actually the decision is arrived at in simple discussions. If too many papers are being classified in this way, or it becomes apparent that there are too many subordinates who have the right to make the classification, it is relatively simple for a President to say, in effect: "Too many people are classifying too many papers for my eyes only, and too many of these papers are not worth my time."

The same comment could be made about "Top Secret" and "Secret" papers. Eventually there are too many of them, and too many people know their content. The more people who know a secret, the less secret it is. In addition, simply taking care of increasing numbers of papers classified at these levels becomes a major burden in the government, because the handling of them is very cumbersome. Someone has to be responsible for such papers; they have to be signed in and out of every office; only designated people may carry them; they must be locked up when not in use.

So, every now and then there is a top level reform in the classifying of confidential papers. The number of subjects that may be so classified and the number of people who may do such classifying is sharply reduced, and everything operates perfectly, for a while. Then, slowly, the old bureaucratic virus takes over and the whole process is repeated.

The problem is increasingly more difficult to handle in the lower classifications, for here the level of classification becomes a matter of personal pride. Whereas at the top level most people are anxious *not* to handle classified papers simply because of the vexing and annoying personal problems of dealing with them, at the lower level it becomes a sort of status symbol to have the power to handle classified official papers.

In United States embassies abroad, much of the non-classified work is performed by employees who are natives of the country involved, or in official U.S.

language, "indigenous personnel." All sorts of non-confidential office work can be performed by such employees, such as assembling trade figures for the commercial attaché's report, or employment figures for the labor attaché's report, or important press stories for the press attaché. For example, Nation X reports that it expects its wheat crop to be so many hundred thousand tons this year, or its unemployment figures to reach such and such, or such and such an important newspaper announces the appointment of a new editor; all this is reported either in government press releases or the newspapers of the country, is duly collected, translated, and collated by the respective sections of the embassy and transmitted to the State Department in Washington. You might ask why the United States government goes to all the expense and bother of maintaining embassies in foreign countries if all this material is available to the public. The answer is that gathering such information is only one of the functions of the embassy, and by no means the most important; more than that, it is much easier for the State Department to make use of such material if it comes in in the same form from each country abroad.

Frequently, however, these reports, after having been prepared by native employees, will be classified as "Restricted." Why, is a complete mystery, except for the previously mentioned sense of importance that a certain type of bureaucrat gets out of stamping a security classification on a paper. The net result of the

classification is that, technically, the native employees
of the embassy had no right to see the papers, though
they were the ones who had prepared them! The folly
is doubly compounded by the fact that everything
contained in the reports was public information,
available to anyone who wanted to bother to read it in
its original form.

But no amount of protesting has ever been able to
make a real dent in this process. It is not cited as a
serious defect in the classification system, simply as an
incident of how the human mind can work when
concerned with classification. The same sort of process
takes place in the offices of the Pentagon and the State
Department, particularly among the staffs. Because
security clearance is directly related to the importance
of the job, it follows that if a man holds a very high
security clearance, he must of necessity hold a very
important job. And, obviously, a man cleared to
handle matters concerned with the very highest decisions of government must in turn have a staff of the
greatest importance.

This kind of status classification impinges on the
general flow of information, and the individual's right
to know, in that it becomes virtually impossible for a
reporter to gain access to information that has been
grossly over-classified merely to bolster the ego of one
man, or to enhance the importance of bureaucratic
staffs.

While sporadic efforts have been made to right this

wrong, and while there is a wealth of material available within the government on the proper method of classifying, no basic reform ever seems to be achieved. The day may come when it will be necessary for the government to establish a classification review board to deal with the problem and undoubtedly this will come about, not to insure a freer flow of information to the American public, but simply because of the inability to handle the mass of classified papers in accordance with security regulations.

It may be noted that the British Official Secrets Act, which rules on the dissemination of classified information in England, provides much stiffer penalties for disclosure than America imposes. In England, it is a crime to publish any classified information from government departments without official clearance. Nevertheless, fewer documents are classified at a high level there.

There is also in the United States another important field of information to which the public is not made privy, yet which does not appear to have any connection whatever with national security.

A perennial example is the U.S. Army testing of motor vehicles. The army subjects to tests parts of vehicles that most mechanics never heard of, and tests them on courses that make the test courses of most automobile manufacturers look like quiet parkways. These tests are conducted so that the army will have the results available when it is ready to buy a few hundred sedans or trucks off the assembly line. We are not talking about such specialized heavy-duty vehicles as tank transporters here. On production-line vehicles, of course, the army does not have the right to order the manufacturer to make modifications, but if it finds that the brakes on Car A begin to fade after ten thousand miles while those on Car B hold for fifteen thousand miles, it naturally will buy its few hundred sedans from manufacturer B.

It is obvious that the results of these army tests might provide a basis of judgment for an ordinary citizen debating whether to buy Car A or B, and reporters have long sought to have the test data declassified so that it can be reported to the general public. But the army maintains that it is authorized to spend the money to make tests only for the army's internal information, and that release of the results of the tests is not covered by the authorization.

It may be just as well, from one point of view. If the army ever issued a report as scathing as Ralph Nader's of some American-made cars, it is not hard to foresee the consequences: top automobile company officials charging down to Washington to protest to everyone from the President down; statements by Congressmen that the army was undermining the free enterprise system; studies showing that building cars to army standards would cut auto production in the United States by 10 percent; other studies showing that thousands of jobs would be lost in the automobile industry, and so on.

There are a substantial number of other products that are tested by various federal agencies such as the Food and Drug Administration. The results of these tests, also, are known only to the agencies involved.

In these cases, as in the army testing of motor vehicles, national security is not used as justification for secrecy; the news embargo is justified instead by the phrase "not in the public interest." But the question is: *Who* determines the public interest?

The new Freedom of Information Act, signed by President Johnson in 1966, was supposed to take away the arbitrary right of government agencies to deny information to the public, or, more specifically, to reporters and historians, and to open the records of public agencies to those concerned persons, but in fact it has not turned out this way.

Professor Allen Weinstein of Smith College, for example, who is writing a history of the so-called "Cold War," went through all the official channels to obtain the Federal Bureau of Information records on Alger Hiss.[2] Of a file of an estimated fifty-three thousand pages, Professor Weinstein received a total of seventeen. "At this rate," said Professor Weinstein, "it will take me 1,040 years to get the material."

Apparently, what the Freedom of Information Act has achieved more than anything else is to establish a legal basis by which, if a government department or official refuses to release government information on what an information-gatherer may regard as captious or insufficient grounds, a suit may be brought, and if the court determines that the grounds are, in fact, captious or insufficient, the court may order the release of the information. It is not a huge step forward, but at least it is a step.

Previously, there was no recourse except to go to a higher ranking person in the department, and hope that he would overrule the first decision, or to try to get the information through other channels. A favorite method was to get a friendly congressman to write a letter to the head of the department in question, asking for the information. The heads of government bureaus do not hastily refuse the requests of congressmen, especially congressmen who may be on an appropriations sub-committee, but it is a cumbersome way of getting information.

Unsatisfactory as the federal Freedom of Information policy may be, there is no parallel to it on the local community level. It is not unusual in many communities in the United States even today for all important decisions to be made in camera. That is, though local community laws may require public hearings on various matters, and the hearings may be held, the governing board generally holds its decision-making sessions in private. There is nothing particularly wrong in this since the public has presumably had its say, provided the board issues a statement on how the decision was made, how it was arrived at, and who voted on each side. In a good many cases, however, boards announce only what the decision was and what the final vote was on each side.

Whether this is a good practice or not can be debated either way ad infinitum. Again, it's a factor of public information that citizens and communities must decide for themselves, and presumably on a case by case basis.

On the one hand, it can be argued, and has been, that if the name of each board member is listed with an indication of how he voted, it will take a considerable amount of political courage for a board member to argue against what he knows is the heavy preponderance of public opinion, even if he is personally convinced that public opinion is wrong.

But on the other hand, it can also be argued that if voting records are always kept secret, it is never really possible for the individual voter to know the pattern of the board member's voting. It is not possible to determine whether he *always* votes from this point of view or that; in other words, to determine his political philosophy, insofar as a voting pattern shows it.

The voting records of all elected officials on the national level, and of a good many on the state level, are compiled and printed—generally around election time—in the newspapers and magazines, so that the voters can make their own estimates of the various candidates. That is possible, however, because votes on national legislation and on most state legislation are recorded in public sessions at which reporters and interested citizens may be present. This is not quite as aboveboard and civic-minded as it might seem at first glance. Most of the shenanigans in bills in Washington, D.C., and in the various state capitals are committed in committee, or away from public buildings entirely, as the investigation of almost every political scandal on record gives ample evidence.

It is done much the same way at the local level except that local politicians can be subject to much more intensive scrutiny than on the higher level.

Eternal vigilance, it has been said, is the price of liberty. It certainly is the price of the closest thing you can hope to get in freedom of information.

It is obvious that the press has come a long way in the past generation in its methods of information-gathering and news dissemination, and even in its levels of responsibility; it is obvious, too, that government certainly has not matched its rate of progress.

6

TRUST OF THE PRESS, TRUST OF THE GOVERNMENT

PERHAPS ONE OF the most valuable services that the press performs for the citizen in today's society is the maintaining of this eternal vigilance for him, when he has neither the time nor the resources to do it personally. You may have the resources to attend your local town or city council meetings, but you certainly do not want to devote your life to going to meetings.

And, while not even the most devoted advocate of the press can argue that the press does a perfect or even a near-perfect job in the way it maintains this eternal vigilance, yet neither is it as irresponsible or biased as its critics—principally its political critics—have charged.

To establish the "person you trust" mentioned earlier, it is necessary also to make a judgment about

the press, about its responsibility, competence, and
fairness in its day-to-day operations as well as on the
broad front already discussed.

It is remarkable how the pattern of criticism of
the press remains unvaried over the years, even the
centuries. All Presidents have complained about the
press from George Washington down to and especially
including Richard Nixon, and so have most political
figures, great and small, in office or out.

In recent months, the public official who most
consistently attacked the performance of the American
press was former Vice President Spiro Agnew.

President Nixon's own deep animosity toward the
press has been apparent on numerous occasions, but
was most appallingly expressed in 1962, on nationwide
television, on the occasion of his admitting defeat in his
campaign for governor of California, when, obviously
so tense and bitter that he could hardly speak, he said
sardonically to the assembled reporters, "Just think
how much you're going to be missing—you won't have
Nixon to kick around any more." As President, except
for a recent outburst directed toward television commentators, Nixon has kept his comments about the
press pretty much to himself, or within his own circle.
True, he did criticize the press coverage during his
most recent campaign, but so did the Democratic
candidate, Senator George McGovern.

Agnew, however, starting late in 1969, began to
deliver a series of vitriolic attacks on the news media,

particularly the television networks, though he by no means omitted such leaders of the "liberal establishment" press (his term) as the *New York Times* and the *Washington Post*, accusing them principally of bias in reporting actions of the Administration.

Agnew's first speech was precipitated by what he called "instant commentary" by television analyzers about a speech on the Vietnam War that the President had just delivered on television. If Agnew had left it at that, he might have found some unexpected friends in the world of television. Some time after Agnew's speech, as a matter of fact, both Eric Sevareid and Howard K. Smith, two well-known news analysts on television, said they both hated doing "instant commentary." Instant commentary means that a well-known television figure appears in the studio and discusses the significance of an important speech by a high official immediately after it has occurred. Smith said, quite reasonably, that he'd prefer to "have a little time to think" before he made any comment.

Agnew's problem was that he didn't know enough to quit when he was ahead, for he went on to lump all the TV networks and quite a number of newspapers and magazines together as part of an "establishment," without appearing to recognize a quality of basic human nature that he, as a practicing politician, should have known better than most. If you have five separate enemies—in this case, the three television networks plus the *Times* and *Washington Post*—the

single, certain way to insure their banding together is
to attack them simultaneously, and on the same basis.
What Agnew forgot was the eternal verity: divide and
conquer.

The weakness of Agnew's approach was perhaps
best analyzed by Kenneth G. Crawford, the columnist
of *Newsweek* magazine. Wrote Crawford:

> The curious thing about Agnew's vehement protests
> is that President Nixon's press has not been all that
> bad. His domestic initiatives have been quite generally
> applauded. The divisive war he inherited has been
> responsible for his troubles with the press. It was
> resentment of the instant TV criticism of the Presi-
> dent's recent speech on Vietnam that set Agnew off.
> Commentator's skepticism about Mr. Nixon's promise
> to withdraw from Vietnam on a progressive, orderly
> schedule was angrily resented.
>
> This resentment was understandable. But it
> launched Agnew on the generalization that TV has
> taken a monolithic stand against the Nixon war
> policies, as though Eric Sevareid and Howard K.
> Smith, who are in complete disagreement about the
> war, broadcast the same line. This was disquieting to
> television managers, whose position is delicate because
> the airwaves they occupy are limited and they are
> Federally licensed. So their replies to Agnew were as
> extravagant as his criticism of them.

It required the most thoughtful of press men—Walter Cronkite, John Chancellor, and Harry Reasoner in
addition to those mentioned above—to argue that
perhaps there had been *some* good in Agnew's attacks,

in that they had forced the media to take a second look at the sort of job they were doing in reporting.

While, as has been said, other Presidents and other high ranking officials have carried on their own vendettas with the press and used such government agencies as the Federal Bureau of Investigation to harass newspaper reporters, there seems to be no doubt that, starting with Nixon's own deep distrust of the press, shared by his top officials, the Administration, unlike all previous ones, began a concerted campaign to destroy its credibility and trustworthiness with as many Americans as possible—the very foundation upon which the press rests.

It is an extraordinary position for any government to find itself in, for it obviously demands a process of ratiocination that is impossible for any logical mind to follow, the antithesis of the entire foundation of democracy or any form of responsible government. The Administration was asking Americans to believe the press when it spoke favorably of the Administration, but disbelieve it when it spoke unfavorably. This is an obvious appeal only to that segment of the population that suspends reason.

The basic difference between the present Administration and previous ones is that, while previous ones may have fulminated against the press, and while it may be an aphorism of politics that "if you're not for us, you're against us," there never before has been a general atmosphere of "if you're not with us, we'll

destroy you," to quote White House aide Egil Krogh.
Politically, this is a perfect example of the totalitarian
mind at work. Chairman Mao, for example, said: "We
will effectively silence the reactionary elements." But
the Administration doesn't seem to realize that in
attempting to destroy others, if trust be the touchstone,
it is destroying itself.

This is an extremely serious problem, as far as the
right to know is concerned, for basically all peoples of
whatever nation or continent, *want* to know and *want* to
believe. It is all very well for us at home to smile at the
words of the dictator of a minor nation who ascribes all
his internal problems to the "imperialist designs" of
the United States, because the American realizes that
this can hardly be so. But the people of that nation
believe it because they *want* to believe it, and because
they must have someone to blame. In this day and age,
the favorite scapegoat is the United States.

It is not at all new for a small country to place the
blame for its troubles on a more powerful one. For
example, Imperial Rome for several hundred years
was blamed for most of the troubles of the western
world, sometimes with considerable justification; and
for a hundred years or so Great Britain was the
scapegoat. But just as these earlier persons believed in
the truth of those charges, so the people of this
mythical nation believe their leader today.

It is one of the tragedies of today's world that
because of these eternal devotions to ideologies even

the most primitive of learning skills are denied to hundreds of millions of peoples.

One of the most impressive of the advances in this electronic age is the orbiting television satellite which permits broadcasting almost simultaneously to any part of the globe. It is now possible to inform great segments of the world's population of news and current events, almost as they happen, but it also may provide courses in reading, writing, and other basic skills.

This is a most exciting possibility. It will not solve all the problems of the world, of course, but what if everyone in the world could read and write?

That is where the matter of ideology comes in. Read what? And in what language?

The United States has one ideology. The Soviet Union has another. Mainland China has a third. And all three of these ideologies, eliminating all others, are at swords points.

Even if the ideologies, for the purpose of world-wide education, could be temporarily put in abeyance, there also remains the problem of language.

Our earth-circling satellite has the capacity to transmit knowledge, but man is incapable of deciding what is to be transmitted, or in which tongue.

One of the most cogent proposals put before the United Nations in an attempt to solve the language problem around the world was that each member nation teach its native tongue as a first language in its public school systems, but that, in addition, one

common language be required in all the schools of all
the world. The proposal has gotten nowhere. Assume
that the first choice is English. Instantly national pride
raises its head. Why not French? It was the international language of diplomacy for centuries. Why not
Spanish? The peoples of an entire continent speak it.
Why not Chinese? And so on.

There is still another problem. For reasons that are
comprehensible, but not apparently logical, people
regard their languages not so much as a means of
communication as a badge of national pride.

In 1937, for example, Ireland declared that hence-
forth its official name was Eire, and required the
teaching of Gaelic in its schools. Yet how many people
in the world can speak Gaelic? When I was serving in
The Hague, a motion was put before the Parliament to
teach Friesian in the public schools in the northern
part of the country. Friesland is the northernmost
province of the Netherlands, and while obviously all of
its inhabitants speak Dutch, they also have a marked
variant of it named for their province. When the
question of teaching it came before the Parliament,
one member remarked sourly: "For God's sake, there
are only about twenty million people in the entire
world who can speak Dutch in the first place and now
they want to teach Friesian, which even I can't
understand. What are we going to do, end up with
everybody speaking his own language?"

There are Biblical fundamentalists who, pointing to

the story of the Tower of Babel in the Old Testament, argue that the differences among languages are a curse put by God on mankind. They make a pretty good case, too.

But even if the language problem is solved, how is the ideological one to be? That is far more difficult.

The examples are endless, no matter what country they are taken from. Only a few months ago, to cite two widely divergent cases, Poland began a campaign against the use of textbooks in the public school system that reflected the ancient, bitter enmity of the Poles and the Germans;[1] and in Ridgefield, Connecticut, a small New England community of some ten thousand persons, the townsfolk were up in arms over the inclusion, in a suggested reading curriculum for students in the junior high school, of the book *Soul on Ice* by Eldridge Cleaver.[2] Ridgefield had previously been involved in a controversy over the removal of books by Robert Frost and Eric Sevareid from the curriculum, so the fact that Cleaver is what is described as "a black militant" was not the key issue. The fact was that Frost and Sevareid were regarded by the townsfolk as "controversial." How a poet and a newscaster can be described as "controversial" is not exactly clear, beyond the fact that neither regards the conditions of human life as perfect, but they were on the list.

And, lest it be thought that discussions or arguments of this nature are carried on only on the high level of proper education for the young, it is but necessary to recall that censorship, destruction, and ceremonial burning of books have existed almost as long as books themselves have existed, and men have been tortured to death for the simple crime of possession of a book. In the Ridgefield case, things never got that bad, but the president of the Ridgefield Teachers Association, a widow named Mrs. Elfrieda Travostino, received a telephone call one day telling her to look out of her front window, because if she did not withdraw the association's support of the books in question the same thing might happen to her or to her children. She looked out and saw her pet dog hanging from a tree by its legs. It demonstrates the virulence to the human spirit that a differing point of view can cause. One of President Johnson's favorite aphorisms was, "Let us reason together," which has been an aphorism of rational men at least since the days of Socrates, but it applies only to reasonable men.

The point at issue in the Ridgefield case was that neither the teachers nor the teachers' association was taking up the cause or even point of view adopted in any of the books listed on the supplemental reading list. The books were simply considered worth reading to demonstrate to the students that there are differing views of American society and of man's lot. In other words, the teachers were performing the highest function of teachers: they were teaching. If the point of education is to teach people to think, or to try to teach them to think, this is what was being done.

One charge against the books mentioned was that they were pieces of "Communist propaganda." The Ridgefield Board of Education saw fit to bow to this pressure by simply eliminating entirely the two courses for which the books were recommended.

This is by no means an isolated case. School boards, like all public institutions, simply focus and magnify the feelings, emotions, and occasionally even the thoughts of the communities in which they exist.

The National Council of Teachers of English, in a pamphlet entitled "Meeting Censorship in the School," cites case histories of censorship and attempted censorship exercised by parents—often individual parents, as opposed to groups—over books that few rational people could object to:

1. Pearl Buck's *The Good Earth*, because it contains a scene describing the birth of a child;

2. J. D. Salinger's *The Catcher in the Rye*, for the use of an "obscene word" three times;

3. *A Pictorial History of the Negro in America* by Langston Hughes and Milton Meltzer and *A Martin King Treasury* in The Negro Heritage Library Series, for a variety of reasons. One is that Hughes's poetry was "atheistic" and another that the authors or their associates were "connected with Communist front organizations."

And a whole raft of other unlikely candidates: *The Diary of Anne Frank* ("pro Jewish"); John Steinbeck's *Travels With Charlie* (Charlie's bladder troubles. Charlie was Steinbeck's pet French poodle who traveled with him); *To Kill a Mockingbird* (profanity); *Little Black Sambo* (no reason given); *Kon-Tiki* (rough language); George Orwell's *1984* (lewd and indecent) . . .

The list could go on for pages, but the point is made.

In free societies, the proscriptions against books are not generally launched by official authorities, but by unofficial, such as those in Ridgefield, which reflect the community's hostility against disapproving views of society as the community knows it. In the United States the foremost politico-social-economic view is the sanctity of the institution of private ownership. Whether this view is a correct one, and a discussion of how different societies deal with it, is not a subject for this book. Here, it is sufficient to point out that virtually from the days of the very first settlers the dream of this country has been the private ownership of land. In the seventeenth and eighteenth centuries the average European who emigrated to the new world had, among other dreams, the one of "becoming his own man," of being able to buy or to settle on land that would become his, something that was an impossibility in his own country. This dream, and the realization of it, is part of the American image of the inviolability of private ownership. It is part of "making your own way," the whole ethic of being independent.

It seems that this dichotomy will forever exist, and simply indicates the problems that exist in dealing with freedom of information. If one group of people are

heart and soul dedicated to the belief that such-and-
such is true, it is very hard, if not absolutely impossible,
for them to accept even the slightest suggestion that
this is not absolute truth. And the problem with trying
to deal with such a belief is that it is built into the very
fabric of the human soul; it seems to come from roots
so deep that they are ineradicable. Some very good
minds have argued that the whole concept of national-
ism is destructive to global understanding and global
peace. Yet it seems to spring from a very basic
existential quality. Even among primitive peoples, the
stranger is automatically the enemy, the strange tribe
is the foe. It is true of the so-called "civilized" nations,
and all through history it has been a fact for the
human race. This fear of strangeness has been carefully nurtured and played upon by the politicians.

In our own society we see this fear of strangeness
working between people of different colors, different
religions, different nationalities, and—in the case of
Ridgefield, Conn.—different views of the values of the
society itself.

Since it is frequently to the advantage of politicians
to play upon these differences, what role does the
communications media play?

Or if, as postulated at the beginning of this chapter,
the preponderance of trust *is* swinging from the
politicians to the press, what role *can* the press play?

A very great one, and perhaps the greatest, is due to
the resources of television. There is certainly no

newspaper of importance in the United States today that would take an editorial position at all similar to that of William Randolph Hearst's fulminations only two generations ago against the "Yellow Peril" nor a radio network that would broadcast the anti-Semitic tirades of the Reverend Charles E. Coughlin, only a little over a generation ago. (Father Coughlin was an ultra-conservative radio broadcaster in the late 1930s who was finally silenced by his own superiors.)

The great advantage that television has is that it can *show* the viewer what it is explaining. Television has gone into the ghettoes and shown to the nation, in all its immediacy, the conditions that exist there; it has gone into the migrant labor camps from Long Island to Florida to California, to show the truth of the lives of America's lowest-paid laborers; it has gone into the backwoods mountains of West Virginia, down into the mines, into prisons.

And the truth of what it has shown cannot be denied.

7

TWO DECISIONS OF THE WARREN COURT

BEYOND THE CONTRIBUTIONS of electronics, a major influence in bringing about today's information revolution has been a series of court decisions, principally the decisions of the Supreme Court of which Earl Warren was Chief Justice, the so-called Warren Court.

There are two areas in which the Warren Court decisions are important to freedom of information. One was a series of decisions that almost consistently struck down local laws and ordinances providing for censorship of information, affecting principally books and motion pictures. It is true that the current court has since ruled that judgment on what is obscene and what is not shall be made on the basis of the "prevailing standards" of morality in individual communities, but—so far, at any rate—there is no evidence that local communities are making a substantial effort

to return to the standards prevailing before the
Warren Court decisions.

The second area of importance affected by the court
was another series of decisions affirming the basic
rights of minority groups to civil justice in all fields,
principally in schooling and voting.

The decisions on censorship are self-evident in their
relation to freedom of information, but the decisions on
minorities give every indication of eventually becoming even more important and far-reaching. For, with
the new and increasing awareness of their own herit-
ages by minority groups, the entire structure of information in this country—from the sort of stories covered
by the news media to the very way that public school
textbooks were written—underwent an unprecedented
and almost unbelievable series of changes.

A comparison made, in preparing this book, of the
types of stories covered by the news media—television
and radio, newspapers and magazines—in the year
1960 and in the year 1970 shows how vast the change
was. For obvious reasons, the only stories considered
here were those in the fields of foreign news, international relations, politics, and stories about minority
groups. There were twice as many stories in this last
category alone—about minority group activities, interests, and movements—in 1972 than there were ten
years earlier, and the trend is still continuing.

In addition to the increased amount of coverage, the
whole tenor of the coverage changed from one of more

or less dispassionate interest to a more sympathetic understanding of the issues. These changes reflect, also, the divergence of the groups involved. The sharpest and most dramatic shift, of course, appeared in the number and tenor of stories concerning blacks.

Newsweek magazine even teamed with the Louis Harris polling organization, which is well known for its political analysis surveys, to prepare one of the first "cover stories" on the black situation in America to appear in a national weekly news magazine—something that would have been unthinkable previously. And in addition to coverage by basically white-run media, the number of black-owned and black-operated magazines, newspapers, and radio stations increased sharply, as did black stature within white-owned media corporations.

But it was not simply the black Americans who began to occupy a more meaningful place in communications in America. Three other groups of citizens who had long been granted only second- or third-class status in the country began to receive greater consideration—citizens of Oriental origin, principally Chinese; citizens of Spanish or Puerto Rican or Mexican origin, principally in California, Florida, and New York; and America's original citizens, the American Indian.

This has led to another major factor in this information revolution: textbooks by the hundreds are being revised for the nation's public school systems, or totally new textbooks are being written, to try to give a clearer and fairer picture of the roles of all of America's minority groups in the making of the nation.

As many experts in the field have pointed out again and again, the importance of the civil rights decisions was not the impact they had on the minority groups, but on the thinking of the nation's controlling white population.

This is vital in considering the importance of the revolution. The earlier textbooks were not, for the most part, written out of malice or a deliberate philosophy of keeping the minorities "in their places." The texts were simply an outgrowth of the intellectual atmosphere in which they were written. They were, again, a product of their times. It was all very well for a Thomas Jefferson or a George Washington to speak their convictions that slavery was morally wrong, and to free their slaves upon their deaths, but they were isolated voices in a society that had come to depend so heavily on slave labor; and the popular feeling that the black man was intrinsically inferior was only confirmed by the voices of the media, from newspapers to books, during and immediately after the Reconstruction era until we find a William Howard Taft, in 1909, making the statement that Africa "hasn't any history at all except that which we trace to the apes." The treatment of the American Indian during the nineteenth century and well into the twentieth is far too well known by now to need any recapitulation here; but it is not as well known that Chinese immigrants were the subject of the contempt of Presidents from Rutherford B. Hayes to Woodrow Wilson.

"I am satisfied that the present Chinese labor invasion is pernicious and should be discouraged. Our experience in dealing with the weaker races—the Negroes and Indians, for example—is not encouraging . . . ," said Hayes in 1879.[1]

"In the matter of Chinese and Japanese coolie immigration I stand for the national policy of exclusion. The whole question is one of assimilation of diverse races. We cannot make a homogeneous population out of people who do not blend with the Caucasian race . . . ," said Wilson in 1912.[2]

Hayes and Wilson were not stupid or insensitive men; they were simply products of their times. And the media of the day, particularly the books written by the scholarly community for use in schools and colleges, reflect the same climate. Indeed, judging from some of the texts of the day, it would seem that the scholars and teachers took the lead in arguing that the Caucasians were somehow divinely appointed to be a superior race of mankind, even though it is today's fashion to lay most of the blame on the less scholarly writers for those stereotypes of Indians, blacks, and Orientals.

Only against that background can the importance of the current trend in writing be measured.

What it means for today's citizens is that while

prejudice and censorship undoubtedly still exist among
fragmented groups of society, from the small individual
sects of the sort that obviously exist in Ridgefield and
other communities, to the educational systems of entire
states, the fact is that the flood of unbiased material
has reached such proportions in recent years that it
seems to bid fair to overwhelm bias, if such a thing is
possible.

Indeed, one of the things that some responsible
leaders of black groups are beginning to worry about is
what may be called a reverse bias, the feeling the
whites once had, that simply being black is somehow
itself inherently good and automatically invests superi-
ority over other groups, say the Jews or the Puerto
Ricans.

This is a totally different topic from the right to
information, however, and is mentioned here only
because it relates to the way in which, in the past, the
subjective writer, convinced of the rightness of his
cause, influenced the validity of information.

What must be guarded against today is that a new
generation of subjective writers does not replace one set
of myths with another equally persuasive. For the
techniques of subjectivity have become far more subtle
than in the old days of Hearst and his blatant
propaganda. In a free society, and for the citizen
desirous of true information, this is one of the most
difficult hurdles to cross. Whether the modern writer is
a true believer in whatever the cause, or simply a paid

propagandist, he achieves his effects not by the exhort-
atory, but by the subtle.

Time magazine of the 1930s was certainly the best
known and possibly the most skillful of the subjective
instruments of information. If it were discussing a
political candidate, for example, the report of what the
candidate *did* and what he *said* might be perfectly
correct; the difference came in the shading of words
and phrases describing what he did. If *Time* favored
the candidate, he "was glowing with confidence" as he
"strode" to the speaker's platform; if *Time* was against
him, his face "was flushed" as he "seemed to half-trot"
to the platform. In both cases it meant that the
candidate was moving fast and that his complexion
was faintly rubicund, but there's a wide difference in
the impression given between a man who is "glowing"
and one who's "flushed."

This technique soon spread from *Time* into the
general press and is now so prevalent that it is a
commonly accepted technique.

The old newspaper dictum about the way in which
to begin a story—that the first paragraph should
contain the salient "five W's," who, what, where,
when, and why—has been in large part replaced by
the opening paragraph that, in a story that concerned
the senseless slaying of twelve persons on a sunny
afternoon, might begin: "At three in the afternoon of a
warm summer day, all seemed peaceful on Main
Street. Every now and then a car passed, and a group

of children were playing softball, six on one side and seven on the other. Then, at precisely 3:12 P.M., the front door opened in a dingy, rundown tenement . . ."

Now, this is a fine opening for a detective story, or for a Sunday feature. But for an account of what happened?

It is odd to realize that the newspapers have borrowed this technique from the news magazines, where it had become a hallmark ("the art of the irrelevant detail," [3] it was once described) for the simple reason that the news magazines recognized from the start that they could not compete with the newspapers as far as the immediacy of their stories went. The average story in a news magazine reports events that happened anywhere from three to six days earlier, and it was in the attempt to cope with this problem that the magazines came to rely almost entirely on what is called "the backward lead."

Its insidiousness lies in the fact that it all but demands subjectivity rather than objectivity in reporting, which is precisely what the more thoughtful critics are concerned about in the midst of today's revolution in communications.

The vast new coverage of all sorts of facets of the American scene that has emerged within the past ten years can be of incalculable value to the individual, provided the picture that emerges is as close to the true one as possible, undistorted either by subjective writing, or, in the case of television, the inclusion of unidentified film tapes made at other times and in other places.

The second area in the communications world in which the court decisions have played so important a role is that of censorship.

Here, newspapers have barely been affected, for the very good reason that virtually the only censorship they are subject to is largely self-imposed. The censorship decisions apply almost exclusively to the other media—books and plays, movies and television.

"No one was ever corrupted by a book," is a saying attributed to the Prohibition-era Mayor of New York, James J. Walker, and it is probably mostly true, but again in the differentiation between the printed word and the electronic medium, there is the difference between the seeing and the doing.

In fact, there is the basic difference between the explicit and the implicit.

The Elizabethans were possibly as bawdy a crew as ever existed in the English-speaking world, but William Shakespeare, who undoubtedly knew them all, did not rely on the use of what are now referred to as four-letter words. This was because Shakespeare understood a basic quality of the human mind, that the unspoken is more poignant than the spoken, that the unseen is more terrible than the seen.

Shakespeare, for example, was able to write most specifically of female attributes and of the pleasures and vagaries of love without the use of "four-letter words," even though he wrote for an audience considerably more earthy than most of today's audiences.

Shakespeare did not impose this self-censorship upon himself out of any sense of prudery. He simply knew that what the audience imagined was far more graphic in each person's mind than he could evoke with the written, or spoken, word.

What he understood was that each person's mind and imagination work differently from all others. When in the first scene of *Romeo and Juliet*, for example, he has Sampson and Gregory discussing the taking of maidenheads, he can hardly be accused of not being forthright, and later in the same play, when he has Mercutio talking about Rosaline's "fine foot, straight leg and quivering thigh and the desmesnes that there adjacent lie," his audience knew perfectly well what he was talking about, and could imagine the delights for themselves.

Similarly, when Conan Doyle wanted to evoke a mood of horror in the Sherlock Holmes story, *The Adventure of the Devil's Foot*, he wrote of a character finding his family in these terms: "His two brothers and his sister were seated round the table exactly as he had left them, the cards still spread in front of them and the candles burned down to their sockets. The sister lay back stone-dead in her chair, while the two brothers sat on each side of her, laughing, shouting, and singing, the sense stricken clean out of them . . .

There is absolutely no explanation of what the horror can be which has frightened a woman to death and two strong men out of their senses . . ." Conan Doyle, in short, doesn't explain the horror or even conjecture at it; he wants the reader to use his own imagination of horror.

The classic film "M" about a child murderer, still sometimes shown on television, won all the awards it did by the use of this sort of suspense: not once is the murder of a child shown. In one classic scene the murderer is seen, from the rear, leading a little girl victim up the stairs to his room. The camera stays at the bottom of the stairs, focused on the door of the room, which is slightly ajar. Presently the little girl's ball rolls out of the room and the camera follows it as it bounces down the stairs and finally rolls to a stop in the corner. That is all. It is left to each person to imagine what happened in the room.

All these are instances of the writer, or film director, deliberately withholding information for artistic purposes.

One of the most famous censorship cases of recent years centered on the publication of *Lady Chatterley's Lover*. But this book cannot be compared to anything that Shakespeare wrote.

It is probable that Shakespeare knew very well that he was writing for a far more sophisticated audience than was D. H. Lawrence. Lawrence wrote for an almost Victorian audience, and therefore made his points by being more specific in terms that an audience of today regards as naive.

Censorship, in other words, is regulated entirely by the times and feelings of the society in which it exists. Anthropologists, for example, have been able to find that even among the most primitive peoples existing today the only sexual organs that must be concealed are those in the crotch. Those, according to the Old Testament, are the ones that Adam and Eve covered once Eve had made her famous blunder and learned about sin.

The change in modern censorship standards, or values, may be seen in the sexual changes even within the past generation.

A generation ago, it was a startling—and generally well-advertised show—that dared to present a naked woman on the stage. (For the purposes of this discussion, "private" shows of one sort or another, as well as the old burlesque shows, are excluded.) And, generally, even this woman concealed her pubic area. But the point is that she was permitted to appear only if she remained perfectly stationary, any movement at all apparently adding to whatever lasciviousness there was.

Then that taboo disappeared, but still there was the taboo that a moving naked woman could not appear in conjunction with a man; then that disappeared until, in the movies and on the stage, virtually the most explicit sex is shown. What effect the 1973 Supreme Court decision will have on this remains to be seen.

The taboo exists today only insofar as television is concerned, and it is here that the ubiquitous nature of the medium is most clearly illustrated.

In other words, the conclusion is, if you want to see a "dirty" movie, or stage show, you pay your money and that is your privilege. Television, however, not only comes directly into the home, but is also subject to a sort of censorship that neither the stage nor movies are. Plays and movies are basically privately produced. Television and radio are a different matter: they come into your home only by virtue of a license issued by the federal government.

In its decision of 1973, the U.S. Supreme Court in effect took cognizance of the fact that, in the long run, it is the people, through their elected local officials, who decide what is to be censored—what is "indecent," what is "immoral," what is "an offense against public decency," to list only a few of the terms for censorship. (The State of Connecticut still has a law on its books under which persons are prosecuted for the offense of "lascivious carriage.") The Supreme Court ruled that the question of censorship was one for local communities to decide for themselves.

"Morality," therefore, as a standard of censorship is one that is very hard to define. There is always the infinite play of the human mind at work, some of the

minds those of geniuses, many more the minds of
the greedy and the prurient.

The great mind of, say a Joyce, produces a work of
art like *Ulysses*, which is at first banned in the United
States because of the explicitness of some of its
language and images. Agreed. The court is following
the temper of the people. Then the ban is lifted—again
following the temper of the people—because the court
has ruled that *Ulysses* is a "work of art," and that what
may be described as the prurient in it is simply being
used for an artistic purpose.

But then, of course, a considerable number of
publishers and writers, recognizing that such books
were now saleable, rushed into print with an almost
interminable series of books designed solely to appeal
to the eternal human curiosity about sex in all of its
manifestations. The purpose of these books, quite
clearly, was simply that of making money by appealing to man's lower instincts.

It is those final three words—"man's lower instincts"
—that pose the whole basic problem of censorship.
Should society invoke censorship to protect man
against these basic interests?

The answer seems to be yes. As the anthropologist
Margaret Mead has pointed out in her early books,
notably *Sex and Temperament*, there are sexual taboos
even among the most primitive of peoples, and therefore presumably humans have held these beliefs from
their earliest existence. Just how and why these taboos

should have originated is not a subject for this book, but the fact remains that these taboos are very real. The habit of covering the genital organs goes back as far as it can be traced; the privacy of the sex act goes back as far. Certainly such taboos do not exist among the lower animals, and it has been argued that these very taboos are part of man's rise to the relatively sophisticated position he now enjoys.

But it is also true that the taboo creates at the same time the temptation to violate it. As Margaret Mead pointed out, though the sexual mores of the primitive tribes certainly seem less inhibitory than the customs that have prevailed in the more civilized world since days of the Puritans, nonetheless violations of taboos, which are the basis of all censorship, occurred with great frequency even among these primitive tribes.

For the purposes of this book it will be useful to break the problem of censorship down into moral censorship and political censorship.

Moral censorship covers not only sexual mores— which are almost always the ones that occur to the human mind first—but a whole host of others. For example, only a few centuries ago, when forks and knives were almost unknown, even the upper classes ate with their hands, or from a spoon. Anyone eating today the way our ancestors did would certainly be the object of censorship by his peers. Our ancestors thought that a bath two or three times a year was enough. Legend has it that Queen Isabella of Spain

had only three baths in her entire lifetime: when she
was born; when she was married; and when she died.
And, indeed, as recently as the nineteenth century, it
was argued that too frequent bathing was debilitating
to the health.

But the various phases of moral censorship, including sexual mores, are not the concern of this book. At
the present moment of history in the United States, it
does not seem that anyone is being deprived of the
opportunity to read a work of literature because of any
veil of censorship.

To take but one example, a great deal has been
made recently of the fact that a number of books,
plays, movies, and television shows have dealt with the
topic of homosexuality, and this has been hailed as a
step toward the elimination of censorship, as indeed it
is. The ancient Greeks, however, would not have
understood this particular facet of modern morality at
all. To them, true love could exist only between two
men. Women, even though some of them wielded great
power and they were by no means as much second-
class citizens as were the women of Victorian England,
for example, were not to be loved in the sense in which
we understand it today. In fact, the entire concept of
romantic love as we know it is relatively new, built
around the romantization of women that began with
the minstrels of the Middle Ages. True love, to
continue to use our modern understanding of the word,
could exist for the Greeks only between men who had

fought in the same battles, shared the same hardships. In fact, the entire modern concept of homosexuality was unknown to the Greeks. It simply did not exist.

In the field of overt moral censorship, there is but one area in which the federal government is playing an active role, and that is in violence on television on children's shows. Here, the Congress has held enough hearings to warn any sensible television producer that he had better tread warily.

It is in the field of politics that the government has taken an active role, in the form of the "equal time" requirement.

It may be worthwhile to note that Congress would never dare attempt to point out to a newspaper publisher that he was reporting too much "sex" news, or "violence" news, or that his news coverage showed a definite political bias; nor would it make such a suggestion to a theater or motion picture producer. Some theaters that operate in part with the help of federal grants already violate any such dicta. But because of the peculiar nature of television, Congress has no such hesitation. Recently, for example, Congress ruled that professional sports games could not be "blacked out" in home cities provided all the stadium tickets had been sold out 72 hours in advance.

With the "equal time" provision, the government is laying strictures on television against a practice that has been tolerated for centuries in the newspaper field. It had always been the assumption that it was not necessary for a newspaper to present two opposite points of view. The old unspoken opinion was that a *newspaper*, in presenting *news*, could not pervert it, and the fact that the paper prints one-half of the news, or one side of it, bothered no one. The presumption was that there were equally biased papers on the other side, and putting the two halves together would make the whole.

Political censorship is easy to recognize, and in almost all its forms. The great political cartoonists from Thomas Nast to Walt Kelly have known censorship in one form or another. When Kelly, for example, in the 1960s, introduced into his comic strip "Pogo" the character "Simple J. Malarkey" as a satire of the late Senator Joseph McCarthy, a number of newspapers simply dropped his strip.

As with the censorship of books, where political censorship does come in to play, it is almost entirely on the local level, and is about as effective. While it is possible for a local school board to ban such a book as *Soul on Ice* in that particular locality, the mobility of people makes such an action almost ineffectual. For to be effective, if it is banned in the schools, then it must also be banned in the local public library. It is possible that this could follow as a logical sequence, but then it must also be banned from the local bookstores. Again, this is possible, but there we leave the realm of possibility, in this country, at least today. The book is on sale in the next town. There are local bannings of books, but so far as can be determined, there are no statewide bannings of books, certainly none nationwide.

Even in school curricula, though, as mentioned previously, there are school boards that ban certain books; still the number of boards that permit books highly critical of America and the American system creates an educational climate that is almost impossible to conceive of in any other country. This does not mean simply the totalitarian countries, where no criticism of any kind would be tolerated, but even such sophisticated countries as France.

In fact, by far the greatest body of censorship in this country today is self-censorship—the limits the media imposes on itself based on its own judgment of what the community at large desires.

Virtually every newspaper in the country, for example, as well as all the television and radio networks, eschew four-letter words, sometimes almost to the lengths of absurdity. Even the most lurid of the nation's tabloid newspapers almost invariably refer to a bride whose marriage has not been consummated as "an unkissed bride."

News media self-censorship of obscene material also hardly seems to be a matter to raise indignation, but news media self-censorship goes a few steps beyond that. For example, while congressmen as a whole are no more intemperate than the general run of men, there are always those members of Congress who drink

considerably more than is good for them and it is not
at all unknown for a congressman at a party to be
obviously intoxicated. They are also victims of other
human failings, but they take considerable pains not to
allow any of these weaknesses to appear in public.

The reporters in Washington, of whatever political
conviction, are generally thoroughly aware of this and
it's not an unusual topic of conversation at the Press
Club bar. But it is very rare for even a muckraking
reporter to print stories about these flaws unless some
incident brings it to such public attention that it
cannot be ignored. There is no conspiracy involved; it
is simply that the political reporters usually feel that a
politician's private life should remain private unless it
affects the performance of his public duty or otherwise
becomes a matter of public concern. A congressman
can get as drunk as a lord in the privacy of his own or
someone else's home as far as reporters are concerned;
it's only when he gets into an automobile accident to
which the police are called, or gets involved in a brawl
in the lobby of a hotel that it becomes a matter of
public interest.

Incidents like these happen far more frequently on
the lower level—in State capitols and in smaller cities
and towns—than they do in Washington, but the same
self-imposed rule of censorship applies.

Should this be a matter of public concern?

Probably not, because, to repeat, this polite self-censorship by the press does not apply if a politician's

personal problems become a matter of public interest.

In addition, public standards for the morality of politicians have slowly but surely become more exacting over the years, and the ever-increasing ubiquity of the news media coverage of politicians is becoming more and more compelling. Eager as the Republicans were for a winning presidential candidate in 1952, after thirty years of not having elected a President of their party, it is unlikely that Dwight D. Eisenhower would even have been considered had he the reputation for drinking that Ulysses S. Grant had.*

It is true that in the past there have been Presidents whose personal lives were very seamy indeed, but that is a matter for history. And the method of dealing with a President who becomes physically incapable of performing his duties is very thoroughly discussed in books on politics.

There is still another kind of news media censorship, however, which recently has been drawing more and more attention, and that is the increasing determination by publishers and editors of the political viewpoints that are to be allowed access to their columns.

It is different from the more or less involuntary censorship that the very exigencies of time and space impose upon every editor. Every newspaper of any size receives millions of words of information every day— from the wire services, from its own reporters and

---

* It should be pointed out that recent historians maintain that Grant was not a drunkard, despite his reputation.

correspondents, from the press releases that deluge newspaper offices, ranging from the elaborate kits of information sent by the major automobile manufacturers upon the advent of the new models each year, to the single sheet of typewritten paper sent in by the president of the local women's garden club.

Every city editor, every day, prepares a list of "city side" stories that he proposes to have his reporters cover and that presumably will appear in the paper. The stories to cover rely entirely on his judgment; he presumably has his job because the paper's editor and publisher have confidence in that judgment. But even the most perfect of city editors, inspired by the highest ideals and desiring only to present as true a picture as he can of the more important events of the day, has to make a judgment on which stories he thinks newsworthy enough to cover, how much space he can give them, and where in the paper they should run. And every editor of any experience is inured to the complaints he receives the next day from people involved in events he did not have covered, from people who think that their views were not properly explained, or were not sufficiently expounded, or who are offended because the story appeared on page 44.

The same situation applies to the national editor, responsible for coverage of the day's events in the nation, and the foreign editor, responsible for similar decisions in the field of foreign affairs.

The problems involved in these decisions are so

clear, and so well known, that no serious charge of the withholding of information can be leveled in the situation.

Most successful editors are also practicing egotists. However much they may make light of it, and they are fond of citing Franklin Roosevelt's successful presidential campaigns despite the fact that few of the nation's newspaper publishers supported him, deep down they really believe in the power of the press and of their own position in that power structure. There can hardly be a reporter alive who has not heard an editor say, at one time or another when his judgment about running a certain story was questioned: "It's news because *I* say it's news." The State Department, in its assessment of the governments of foreign countries, has long maintained lists of what it calls "opinion leaders." These are the people, the Department believes, who, when they speak, are listened to by the rest of the nation, and high on all these lists, second in importance only to the nations' political figures in most cases, have been newspaper editors.

This psychological quirk is not entirely bad, provided it is kept within the bounds of reason, but it is well to be aware that it exists.

The modern development, against this background, that has disturbed thoughtful critics of the press is the so-called "editorial advertisement." This is an advertisement purchased generally by a group of persons who wish to present their point of view, and one of the

best known—in legal circles—of such advertisements
was one printed in *The New York Times* of March 29,
1960 (at a price of $4,800) to support non-violent
demonstrations by Southern blacks to achieve their full
constitutional rights. The ad was signed by a group of
sixty-four persons ranging from Mrs. Franklin D.
Roosevelt to Harry Belafonte, in general sixty-four
persons about whose concern for civil rights and
personal integrity there could be no question.

But the ad stated, in documenting its case of the
violation of black rights in the South, that during a
demonstration at Alabama State College in Montgomery, the campus was "ringed" by armed police; the
entire student body, in retaliation, refused to re-regis-
ter at the college, and that then, in counter retaliation,
the college dining room had been locked in an effort to
starve the students into knuckling under.

One of the three city commissioners of Montgomery,
a man named L. B. Sullivan, first wrote to the *Times*,
pointing out that these three specific charges were
incorrect—because the events never happened—and
asking for a retraction. The *Times* refused on the
grounds that the charges had been made in an
advertisement and saying, in effect, that it had nothing
to do with it. Sullivan then sued the *Times* for libel.
The case became so complicated that it ended up
before the Supreme Court.

The *Times* presented what many thought was an
extraordinary defense. Whereas previously it had more

or less disavowed the ad as being simply a part of its paid advertising content, over which it had no real control, it now argued that it was an "editorial advertisement," and so fell under the protection of the First Amendment and had all the privileges of free criticism of the government.

The Court found in favor of the *Times*, asserting that the *Times* had printed the ad "without malice."

While this may seem like an abstruse legal problem of interest only to lawyers and newspapermen, it leaves the reader under a total misapprehension.

There can be no question as to the morality of the issues involved. Despite Mr. Sullivan's protestations, made in good faith as they presumably were, there can hardly be any doubt in the mind of any sensible persons that the constitutional rights of blacks in the South have been sorely repressed for at least four generations, and that the city of Montgomery has been a prime offender, whatever recent progress may have been made. Nonetheless, the fact remains that those particular facts in that particular advertisement were incorrect.

To get away from such momentous issues, suppose that in a local political campaign a similar tactic were employed—that a local group took a similar advertisement in a local paper making false allegations against an elected public official. Under the Supreme Court ruling in the Sullivan case, the official would have no recourse.

Congress, indeed, has been so disturbed by the trend to a one-viewpoint press, that it has had before it a bill "to impose on newspapers of general circulation an obligation to afford certain members of the public an opportunity to publish editorial advertisements and to reply to editorial comment." [4] That such a bill will pass within the foreseeable future is extremely unlikely, but it would not seem too much to suggest that a newspaper that prides itself on fairness as much as the *Times* does—and with considerable justification— should take the step of checking the facts in its political advertisements to the extent that it does for its commercial ads. If it cannot, it should allow the same rights of rebuttal, or at least provide the opportunity to set forth the facts correctly, just as it would in the case of one of its own office-written editorials.[5]

An extremely important area in which enormous strides have been made against censorship in recent years has been in the field of the undergraduate press, principally in colleges, but also to a certain extent in high schools.

Students have always, and rightfully, been rebels against the status quo, but college newspapers—of which there are approximately fifteen hundred in the nation—have generally been rather tame, devoting more space to the fortunes of the football team and the food in the cafeteria than to questions of greater substance. There have been notable exceptions to this generalization, but usually these have been the papers

published by the Ivy League and other privately
endowed colleges. The undergraduate papers published in the land grant and other publicly supported
colleges, by far in the vast majority, form the basis for
the generalization.

Actually, the Supreme Court has been granting full
citizenship rights to students for far longer than most
people, except constitutional lawyers, realize. It was as
far back as 1942, for example, in the full fervor of
World War II, that the Supreme Court ruled that
children were not compelled to salute the flag in
school; in 1969 the court ruled that students had the
right to express political opinions during school hours.

The turning point for the freedom of information for
undergraduate newspapers came in 1967, when the
president of the University of Alabama, Dr. Frank A.
Rose, had become something of a *cause célèbre* around
the state because he had been criticized by some state
legislators for not ruling over student publications at
the university with a strict enough hand. Dr. Rose had
defended his own position, and the controversy had
been widely reported in the regular newspapers of
Alabama and other southern states.

At this juncture, Gary Clinton Dickey, the youthful
editor of the college newspaper published at Troy
State College, a small college at Troy, Alabama,
decided to run an editorial supporting Dr. Rose's
position.

As explained by Melvin Mencher, journalism professor at Columbia University, Dickey was aware that he was probably heading for trouble and so first showed the editorial to the head of the English department (who said he thought it looked all right), then to his faculty advisor (who said he didn't), finally to the college president, Ralph Adams, who—reasoning that the state legislators and the governor controlled the college's budget and therefore were de facto owners of the paper and could not be criticized by it—told Dickey not to run the piece.

Dickey didn't. Instead, he ran the headline of the editorial, "Lament for Dr. Rose," and in the empty space below where the editorial would have appeared he ran the legend "Censored."

The paper was confiscated, Dickey was fired as editor, his student loan was withdrawn and, during the summer, he was advised by the dean of men that it had been voted "not to re-admit him at this time."

Dickey went to court. Federal District Court Judge Frank M. Johnson, Jr. ruled that the expulsion was in violation of the First and Fourteenth Amendments of the Constitution, and ordered Dickey reinstated.

Professor Mencher, writing about this case in the October 1972 issue of *The Quill*, a magazine devoted to undergraduate publications, ended by saying: "Clearly, the seventies began a new era for the campus press. It could only look to itself for its success or failure as an instrument of information and change on the campus."

It is apparent from Judge Johnson's decision that the Bill of Rights is not confined to the rights of adults.

Obviously, the rulings of the Warren Court are affecting the most venerable and prestigious examples of the press as well as the newest and least well known.

8

SECRECY

THERE IS NO REASON to believe that the government vs. press battle over secrecy is anywhere near its end. Indeed, within the next few years the fighting may be the hardest. If there is one thing that the Pentagon Papers made clear, it is that far too many government decisions have been made in secrecy.

Professor Arthur M. Schlesinger said that the "secrecy system has become much less a means by which government protects national security than a means by which government safeguards its reputation," [1] and A. M. Rosenthal, managing editor of *The New York Times*, discussing the Pentagon Papers, said "they show clearly that one administration after another carried itself and the country into a constantly escalating series of wars . . . and that each step was taken because the government knew that the preceding step had failed. Yet the public never knew that each step had failed." [2]

This excessive secrecy is also of fairly recent develop-

ment. It is hard to analyze it exactly, for, like so many
other attitudes of government, it *is* an attitude. The
areas that properly merit secrecy are relatively small
and have been well defined. The new attitude seems to
have simply grown.

Its beginnings, as far as may be determined, arose in
the administrations of President Eisenhower. The
explanation suggests itself that Eisenhower remained a
military man, in his thinking, through both his terms.
This, in one way, was an advantage to the country, for
Eisenhower understood very clearly the workings of
the military mind. To him the title "commander in
chief" was not a sort of honor that went along with the
office of the presidency. To him it meant that when he
told a five-star general to jump, he jumped.

Further, the reaction of the military mind is, when
threatened, attack. Eisenhower knew that, and knew
better. In 1954, for example, he had no hesitancy in
overriding the Chairman of the Joint Chiefs of Staff,
Admiral Arthur W. Radford, in the matter of supplying American military manpower to aid the French in
Indo-China. Dien Bien Phu, the last French strong-
hold in the country, fell to the Communists in May of
that year. At the same time, Eisenhower warned
against committing American ground troops in Asia.[3]
An axiom of western military leaders ever since the
days of Napoleon has been never to get involved in a
ground war in Asia. The distances are incredible and

the manpower is inexhaustible. It may be a pity that Kennedy, Johnson, and Nixon never went to West Point.

Eisenhower, however, made use of his military training in the running of the White House. He introduced the staff system whereby he surrounded himself with trusted aids so that it became virtually impossible for anyone except a Cabinet minister to see him without having first gone through his staff. Nixon revived a similar system when he assumed the presidency.

And Eisenhower would not tolerate a man who discussed, outside the White House, confidential matters that had been brought up in his presence.

Thus, perhaps, all unwittingly, the atmosphere of secrecy was born.

It relaxed considerably during the presidency of John F. Kennedy, though it still existed, and increased slightly during the presidency of Lyndon B. Johnson, though not nearly to the height it had attained under Eisenhower and the even greater height under Nixon.

In large measure, the atmosphere of secrecy is created by the personality of the President. It is sometimes forgotten, though it ought not be, how much the personal character of a President has to do with the way the office of the presidency is conducted.

In President Eisenhower's case, secrecy was thrust on him by his long years of military training and service; Kennedy was an outgoing man by nature, and

only as secretive as a prudent practicing politician who
rises to the presidency need be. Johnson personally was
more secretive than Kennedy, but that was in his
nature; Nixon has carried his demand for secrecy far
beyond the bounds of any President within recent
memory.

If it were simply a matter of the President, that
would be bad enough; but the atmosphere of secrecy is
infectious. A President is not simply a man who sits in
the White House and acts upon recommendations
presented to him by his staff, or by his Cabinet, or by
Congress. He is enormously important in his own
right; if it is in his nature to be secretive, that infects
his entire staff and office. For being on the staff of the
President, or in his office, gives a man a sense of
importance. There are, after all, few people in the
United States who can say: "The President says . . ."
or "The President wants . . ." or "The President told
me to tell you . . ." and have people listen.

There is before Congress at this writing an Adminis-
tration-approved bill for revision of the Criminal
Code, several provisions of which, taken together,
according to Senator Edmund S. Muskie of Maine,
constitute an "Official Secrets Act" similar to the
British one but tougher.[4]

The four provisions would:

1. Punish government officials who disclose military
and foreign policy information, whether its disclosure
would endanger national security or not.

2. Punish newsmen for receiving such material unless they reported it to the government, and returned the material to a government official immediately on recognizing it.

3. Punish responsible officials of publications or broadcasting companies which made such information public.

4. Punish government employees who knew of any unauthorized disclosure and failed to report it.

Senator Muskie points out that no such controls were proposed even during the height of World War I or II, and he argues that:

> Under this proposal, a reporter who catches the government in a lie, who uncovers a fraud, who unearths examples of monumental waste could go to jail—even if he could show, beyond any question, that the government had no right to keep the information secret and that its release could not possibly harm national defense.[5]

As if this proposal were not dangerous enough to the right of information, the law would make the disclosure of *any* classified information a crime; it further defines classified information as:

> Any information, regardless of its origin, which is marked or designated pursuant to the provisions of a statute or executive order or a regulation or rule thereunder, as information requiring a specific degree of protection against unauthorized disclosure for reasons of national security.

In view of the bureaucratic tendency, discussed earlier, to over-classify everything on the "better be safe than sorry principle," even down to and including newspaper stories that have already been published, it does not take much imagination to realize that it is clearly the Administration's intention, if it can, to make the press entirely dependent on its own press releases and publicity handouts. And, so far, no one has surfaced in the present Administration characterized by the candor that marked Fiorello LaGuardia, late mayor of New York, who once admitted: "When I make a mistake, it's a beaut."

In addition, the penalties that the proposed new law would impose are truly staggering: from three to seven years in jail, and fines that could aggregate $50,000. In contrast, the present information-security program, which basically derives its authority from executive order, provides no such penalties; the worst that can happen to a government employee is an official reprimand or transfer to a different position.

Actually, the Administration position on using the courts to assist in the concealment of information was clearly indicated even before the Senate hearings on Watergate began, while the investigation was still going on.

The most dramatic clue was offered in March 1973, when a Federal district court in Washington issued subpoenas to at least a dozen newspaper and news magazine reporters, editors, and executives—on behalf of the Committee to Re-elect the President—for "all documents, papers, letters, photographs, audio and visual tapes . . . which relate in any way to the break-in at the Democratic National Committee headquarters . . ." [6]

If honored, those subpoenas would have put into the hands of the Committee for the Re-election of the President, or CREEP, as it came to be known, every private and confidential record of all the reporters, editors, and executives cited, the names of all their sources, and everything that had been said during the interviews. The publications involved did not comply. The *New York Times*, the *Washington Post*, and *Time* magazine moved to have the subpoenas quashed; the *Washington Star-News* said its reporter would answer the subpoena, but would not turn over private notes. But the point of danger, as far as freedom of information is concerned, is that a federal court would issue such an all-sweeping injunction.

The cases cited earlier, on which the Court ruled that a newsman could not refuse to answer questions before a grand jury, involved criminal procedures. The records and papers ordered subpoenaed in the Watergate case, however, related solely to a civil matter: the re-election committee wanted the records in order to establish civil damage cases against leading Democratic figures who, the committee said, had made libelous statements about Republicans concerning the break-in.

It is unthinkable that such a development could ever come to pass. What the judicial arm of the government is requiring by such decisions as these is that the reporter—whose immunity so far has rested basically on the fact that he is a member of the fourth estate and is, actually, the representative of the people in investigating the facts in any given case, including mistakes, deceptions, and felonies committed by the government—would now be required to use his special status for the purpose of acquiring information that the government itself is incapable of obtaining. The precise legal status of CREEP in recruiting a federal district judge to issue subpoenas on its behalf, has never been made clear.

In other words, a reporter enjoys his special status precisely because people know that he does *not* represent an arm of the government and that if he promises not to quote them, or offers some other guarantee of immunity, that word will be honored.

It comes down, again, to the matter of trust. But what would happen if it turned out that the courts could *order* the reporter to violate his confidence?

Obviously, the reporter's word would no longer be sacrosanct and there would be no way in which the reporter could gain the confidence of the people whose best interests he is presumed to be representing.

Against these actions by the Administration, there is a counter-tide. The Congress itself is trying to draft some sort of bill that would give protection of information to newsmen. As mentioned earlier, newsmen themselves cannot agree on what sort of protection they want, and at a hearing on this topic last year (1973) before the Senate Judiciary Committee, Senator Sam J. Ervin Jr. of North Carolina, who is also chairman of the Senate Watergate committee, remarked to a witness that: "I can argue either side without convincing myself very much either way. This is the most difficult field I've ever had to write a bill in." [7]

An "absolute" shield bill—making *all* of a reporter's information confidential—has already been introduced into the upper house by Senator Alan Cranston of California, and Senator Edward M. Kennedy of Massachusetts. Under it, newsmen would not be required to reveal the sources of any information for news stories. Actually, some fifty bills have been introduced in Congress requiring protection of one sort or another for newsmen.

Such a provision would go far beyond the protection now given a priest or a lawyer. Generally, a priest is absolved from being required to testify about anything said to him in a confessional, and a lawyer may not withhold any information about a client's intention to commit a crime.

But the newspaper columnist James Kilpatrick thinks that such a law would be unconstitutional. It "could result in intolerable violations of the right of a defendant under the Fifth and Sixth Amendments,"

Kilpatrick says.[8] (The Fifth, of course, provides that only a grand jury may indict a person for a capital crime; the Sixth gives a defendant the right to be confronted with the witnesses against him and provides for a compulsory process for obtaining witnesses in his favor.)

Senator Ervin, though sourly commenting that "537 Congressmen aren't going to agree with a bill with a lot of exceptions," nonetheless introduced a bill that would protect a newsman from being required to name his sources if he had promised anonymity to those sources unless he had "actual personal knowledge which tends to prove or disprove the commission of the crime charged or being investigated." [9]

Of that bill, William Thomas, editor of the *Los Angeles Times*—which estimated that it has spent $200,000 in lawyers' fees in the last three years fighting thirty actual subpoenas and fifty more that were threatened—remarked with equal sourness: "We'll go on spending our time in the courts." [10]

Representatives of the press, however, are unanimous in their opposition to the provisions protecting government security in the proposed revision of the Criminal Code. On the one hand, as already explained, it would make reporters entirely dependent on government press releases, which could very well lead to a total apathy about government information and which inevitably would drive reporters to the opposite course of accepting as true any information about government operations that came from a non-government source. Indeed, according to Robert H. Phelps, who is the news editor of the Washington bureau of the *New York Times*, that is already happening. When a non-government source "leaks" information, Phelps said, at a conference sponsored by New York University's Center for International Studies, "we tend to believe it, we tend to play it up." [11]

There is little doubt that the government handling of the information problem during the Vietnam War contributed greatly to the thinking of the Justice Department when it helped to frame the proposed new Criminal Code.

For, during the Johnson administration, the principle of the off-the-record briefing began to be violated.

The off-the-record briefing began during the Franklin Roosevelt administration, and its purpose at first was honorable. To explain it, and its function, let us assume that, say, the Secretary of the Army (back in Roosevelt's day) holds a press conference on an important matter. All reporters then, and now, understand that a Cabinet minister *has* to be a spokesman for the Administration in which he serves, and that the Secretary very well understands that every word he says is an official word, reported around the world. But by the time of the Roosevelt administration, governmental issues had become so complicated and so involved that frequently it was impossible to resolve the substance of them during a press conference. In previous administrations, when life and government were simpler, if a conscientious reporter didn't feel that he had a firm grip on the situation, he could go privately later either to the Secretary or to one of his top assistants and say: "Look, tell me, off the record, what did that *really* mean when the Secretary said he was going to do this. . . . that . . . or the other thing?" And normally, the Secretary or his top assistant would say: "Well, off the record, what it really means is . . ." When the reporter's story came out, it would read: "A highly placed government source later said that the Secretary's statement really meant that . . ."

All perfectly clear and aboveboard. The reporter had a clear story for his readers, and the Secretary hadn't compromised any position he might want to take.

During the first Roosevelt administration, government operations became so complicated, and press coverage in Washington had increased so much, that this one-man relationship between the reporter and the government officer began to be no longer feasible, and the off-the-record briefing was born. The briefing was normally held immediately after the official press conference and was simply designed to allow a group of reporters to get the real story rather than doing it on a man-to-man basis.

The usefulness of this sort of briefing was that the briefing officer told the truth. Of course, being a government employee himself, no briefing officer would ever dream of answering yes if he were asked: "Well, when the Secretary said that, was he really just trying to cover up?" But he would say: "Well, now, look at the problem yourself. Of course the Secretary isn't trying to cover up. But if you were faced with this situation, wouldn't you try to explain that . . ."

The reporters generally got the idea.

During the Vietnam War, however, it slowly became apparent that the briefing officers themselves were either sadly deluded, or they were lying. No commanding officer in the military in any army at any time will admit, especially to a group of reporters, that he sees nothing ahead except disaster. And, of course, no briefing officer is ever going to contradict his superior. But, previous to the Vietnam War, a briefing officer could say: "Well, what the general said is true, of course, but it's also true that the resistance up there is a little heavier than we really expected, and it's taking time to reduce that resistance."

Every reporter with an ounce of experience at his command could guess what that meant without having it spelled out for him.

Newspaper coverage of the Vietnam War was further complicated by the very nature of the fighting. Unlike World War II, or even the Korean War, it was essentially a guerrilla war. There were no fronts nor any clearly defined battle lines. Theoretically, the military is responsible for the safety and protection of the correspondents assigned to it, for correspondents are forbidden by the Geneva convention from carrying weapons, just as are medical personnel and members of the chaplain corps.

Even in a more or less organized war like World War II military authorities don't really like correspondents who go forward of a division headquarters, not because they are trying to cover anything up but because a division is the lowest level of army command that can offer adequate protection to a non-combatant.

Good correspondents, however, have always been willing to forgo army protection for the sake of getting a true picture of how the fighting is going in a particular area, and this was true in Vietnam as it had been in previous wars. By going up into the combat areas the Vietnam War correspondents discovered that the briefings they had been recciving were not the truth. Then the immediate—and natural—surmise was that their travel had been restricted not because of any overweening military regard for their safety, but to conceal from them the fact that the war was going very badly indeed.

Even military writers back in the United States, whose experience had taught them to be very wary of taking military reports at their face value, were surprised at exactly how badly the war was going. These writers, drawing on the lessons of World War II, had been loath to accept air force reports of the effectiveness of their high-level bombing. Official studies after World War II had made clear that the

high-level bombing of combat troops is almost totally
ineffectual and that the effect of such bombing on fixed
military installations—military encampments, troop
concentrations, railroad marshaling yards and war
materiel factories—is almost always highly exagger-
ated. But these writers were not prepared for the
reports on how little real damage to troops or to these
installations had been achieved by bombing in Vietnam, nor the reports of how many wrong targets had
been hit.

All in all, the Vietnam War did a great deal to
undermine the faith of reporters—and, in turn, the
public—in the truth of military reports. It turned out,
indeed, that not only were some field commanders
lying to reporters, they were also sending false reports
back to Washington, which is about as heinous an
offense as an army officer can be accused of.

The Vietnam War, therefore, has dealt a serious
blow to the usefulness of the off-the-record briefing.

What the Justice Department is currently proposing, however, would be a far more savage blow to
government-press relations, for it not only would
penalize government employees who make mistakes,
but also the newsmen who report them. Taken together with the use by the Administration of federal
agencies—such as the Federal Bureau of Investigation,
the judiciary, and the Internal Revenue Service—to
harass newsmen, this begins to look like one small step
along the road that repressive governments walk. Juan

Peròn, for example, in his first term of tenure as President of Argentina from 1946 to 1955 effectively silenced the press as a critic of his regime. If you read the article on the press in the Argentine Constitution, however, which says the Parliament is "forbidden to pass laws calculated to restrict freedom of the press," you would assume that the country must enjoy virtually complete freedom of information. Immediately upon his return to office in 1973 Peron promptly dissolved an American news agency—the Associated Press—which had, over the years, built up an effective news syndicate within Argentina itself.

The present United States legislative-legal assault on the press is only one phase of the freedom of information battle; the administration has also made a number of repressive threats against broadcasters.

The principal threat was in a speech delivered by Clay T. Whitehead, director of the White House Office for Telecommunications policy, before the Indianapolis Chapter of Sigma Delta Chi, the professional journalism fraternity, in December 1972. In the course of this speech, Whitehead, while explaining an Administration-sponsored bill to liberalize license-renewal applications for radio and television stations, attacked the "balance and objectivity" of television network news programs, and accused them of "ideological plugola" and "elitist gossip." Under the new legislation, he warned, local stations would be held totally responsible for the news content of any programs they broadcast, even if the news programs were furnished by one of the major networks.

At nearly the same time, it was disclosed that the White House maintained a continuous monitor-watch on television and radio news broadcasts, and rated the announcers, commentators, channels, and stations as to whether they were pro-administration, neutral (which meant not quite so favorable), or hostile (which meant all other). Now, it was not the monitoring that disturbed the press. After all, since the days of Franklin Roosevelt, someone on the White House staff had been charged with going through the nation's important newspapers every day and listening to newscasts for the purpose of preparing a summary of news stories of interest to the President, including the amount of space given to each story. Monitoring was later expanded, in the Eisenhower administration, to include television programs.

This is eminently sensible. It is one of the President's ways of keeping in touch with the pulse of the country, and no President can afford to spend the time reading all the papers or looking at all news programs himself.

But the Nixon administration was the first to "rate" stations and broadcasters. It was a variant of this approach that caused one of the furors over the so-called "Watergate tapes," when it was revealed that President Nixon was taping conversations and telephone calls in his office, unknown to the speaker.

Again, the practice of taping important conversations is not new, but previously the speaker would be told that his words were being recorded.

Whitehead's speech, together with the revelation of the White House rating system, made a clear inference that the broadcasting industry was quick to catch.

"What Whitehead is saying," said Reuven Frank, president of news for the National Broadcasting System, "is 'We're holding the station accountable for what we don't like to see on each station, and the station's license is involved.' That's quite a threat." [12]

In fact, the license-renewal legislation proposed by the Administration included two provisions that the broadcasting industry had been lobbying for for years: It would have granted licenses good for five years instead of the present three, and it would have provided that the Federal Communications Commission could consider a competing application for a station license only after it had revoked, or failed to renew, the old license.

But this concession to the industry was lost in the storm over Whitehead's speech.

Fred Friendly, a former president of the Columbia Broadcasting System's news division and present advisor to the Ford Foundation on public television, said the proposal could be "the most dangerous thing to come along in fifty years of broadcasting." [13]

"Such legislation," Friendly said, "would make

political footballs out of broadcasters' licenses, to be taken away or granted according to the whim of the political party in power."

And Nicholas Johnson, himself a member of the FCC—though the maverick of the body, more often than not—said the proposed bill in its context "appears to be designed to assure the renewal of individual broadcast licenses, if only they will help bring the networks back in line." [14]

Mistrust, however, as this whole attitude of the Administration showed, begets mistrust.

The fact emerged that the people as a whole, and especially young people continued basically to trust the press and to lose confidence in the Administration. In a Gallup poll in July 1973, a question was posed regarding readers' confidence in newspapers.

Overall, 15 percent trusted them "a great deal," 24 percent "quite a lot," 39 percent "some," 15 percent "very little," and only 4 percent "none." The remaining 3 percent had "no opinion." Of people interviewed in the eighteen to twenty-four-year age group, the comparable figures were almost the same: 16, 25, 39, 15, and 5 percent.

The same poll offered some interesting figures on trust in other national institutions. With the Supreme Court, for example, the trust of young people ran higher than the national average. The figures were, for all people, 20 percent "a great deal," 24 percent "quite a lot," 28 percent "some," only 12 percent "very little," and 5 percent "none." Among the young people, the figures were 25, 26, 33, 8, and 2 percent.

The figures for trust in Congress were, for everyone, 15 percent "a great deal," 27 percent "quite a lot," 36 percent "some," 11 percent "very little," and 3, "none." Among young people (those below 25 years of age), the figures went 13, 29, 35, 14, and 2 percent.

This was the same poll, incidentally, that showed President Nixon, following Watergate, at his lowest ebb of popularity since taking office. His highs, when 68 percent of the population approved of the way in which he was handling the presidency came in November 1969, when the first big contingency of American troops had already been withdrawn from Vietnam and just after he had made a nationwide television speech appealing for support of his Vietnam policy; and in January 1973, when the United States-Vietnam peace had been signed.

But by July 1973, his popularity had dropped considerably: 40 percent of the general population approved of his handling of the presidency, 49 percent disapproved, the rest didn't know. Among younger people, 39 percent approved, 53 percent didn't, 8 percent had no opinion. And by March 1974 *Newsweek* magazine was writing that Mr. Nixon's popularity had slid to a dolorous 27 percent in a new Gallup poll, and his hold on his own party had been badly damaged by two demoralizing by-election defeats in Pennsylvania and Michigan.[15]

There is no telling at this writing what the political future holds for President Nixon as a result of Watergate, including even the actuality of impeachment. But there is no doubt that regardless of any action by Congress, or any final judgment on his popular standing by the public opinion polls, Nixon's reputation has been irretrievably tarnished by the dirtiest political scandal in this country in the last fifty years.

In the final analysis, President Nixon has only himself to blame. An attitude of mistrust begets mistrust. An insistence on secrecy inexorably leads to the question: what is it that is being held secret?

9

THE SUMMING UP

IT HAS BEEN emphasized again and again how complicated the entire question of freedom of information
really is. As Senator Ervin remarked: "This is the most
difficult field . . ." and so it is. For it has no absolutes.
No one man, or even one body of the ablest men, can
say, "This and this should be done," with the absolute
certainty that a chemist has when he says: "If you mix
two parts of hydrogen and one of oxygen, you get
water."

So, the matter of freedom of information is, and will
continue to be, a matter of continuing debate and
conflict.

And, in this day and age, the problems have been
almost unbelievably multiplied by the very complexity
of the world in which we live. There are the political
facts of our everyday lives, the emergence of new
nations around the world, the emerging strengths of
minority groups within our own society, and beyond

that the technical revolution, largely within the last ten years, in the field of communications.

Where does that leave the poor average citizen who, if he wishes to function as an intelligent being and play his proper role in society to the best of his ability, must attempt to cope with these conflicting concepts?

It should be repeated, as said at the very beginning, that the government does and should have areas, clearly defined by law, in which its information should be privileged for a greater or lesser length of time. The State Department's length of classification for documents relating to international negotiations, for example, seems excessive. But that does not mean that the government should be allowed to classify one and all of its millions upon millions of records and to make it a criminal offense to disclose, or to possess, one of those classified papers.

Who is to be the arbiter? At the moment, Congress is; but it would seem that the day must come, within the foreseeable future, when a body representing the three principal interests—the government, the press, and the public—will be given the authority to examine the entire United States security-of-information program (excluding, perhaps, papers in the "Eyes Only" and "Top Secret" categories, which are concerned with still-existing problems) and at least to make recommendations for downgrading the present mountain of classified documents. As any experienced foreign service or military officer can testify, almost all papers in the classifications of "Confidential" or "Restricted" contain information that is either (1) of general public knowledge anyway; (2) outdated, or (3) shouldn't have been classified in the first place.

And, as far as the government's position is concerned, the two danger spots looming clearly ahead in the field of freedom of information are the provisions of the revised Criminal Code and other attempts to make normal news inquiries into federal operations criminal offenses, plus the government's concerted campaign against the rights of newsmen through the use of subpoenas, jail sentences, and other harassments.

On the side of the media, it also should be recalled that each has its defects. The most dangerous weakness in the field of newspapers is the continuing trend toward monopoly journalism, the all-devouring growth of newspaper chains. There is obviously nothing that the individual can do about this and Congress has given no indication that it considers the business maneuverings of newspaper publishers a matter of public concern. It is different in England. In the early 1960s, when two of Great Britain's press lords—Cecil Kind and Roy Thomson—were bidding against each other for ownership of the *London Daily Herald* and the Sunday newspaper *People*, the storm that was raised in Parliament reached the point that the Prime Minister, Harold MacMillan, appointed a Royal Commission to

investigate the development. The government, Mac-
Millan said, was concerned about the reduction of "the
number and variety of voices speaking to the public
through the press." [1]

This monopoly journalism exists—as has been
pointed out—in all but a handful of cities throughout
the United States, and it behooves the reader in the
average city to read his newspaper in the full knowledge that he is getting one point of view, and, all too
often, only one set of facts.

Television, and to a lesser extent radio, has its great
virtues and its great defects. Its great plus value, of
course, is its immediacy. Much of its information on
news programs is first hand. The viewer is taken into
the Senate hearing room; he is taken into the halls of
political conventions, and frequently into the streets
outside. As far as supplying immediate and exact
information goes, television has no peer.

Its great defect is that, because of this very immediacy, it tends to emphasize the sensational even more
than newspapers. There is not a newspaper or reporter
alive who has not heard the questions: "Why do
newspapers have to be so sensational? Why do they
always print the bad news? Aren't the people who live
decent lives just as important as the people who
murder somebody?" The answer is, certainly those
people are as important and, for the one person in a
hundred who commits a serious crime, society may

bless itself that it has ninety-nine who do not. But the answer lies in the old trite newspaper saying: "When a dog bites a man, that's not news; when a man bites a dog, that is." When Demosthenes' Athenians went about asking what was new, they didn't want to be told "Absolutely nothing."

In the field of television, the viewer, because of its immediacy, is much more at the mercy of the producer or the editor than is the newspaper reader. If a newspaper reader, for example, is revolted by the details of a heinous crime, he can turn to the next page and read about the prediction of the wheat harvest, or turn to the sports pages, or read the comics. The television viewer has no such alternative. If he wants to see the news, this is the news program. If the program happens to consist of a campus sit-in, a race riot, and a peace demonstration, the viewer gets the distinct impression that the whole country is coming apart at the seams. The fact that of the nation's 5 million college students, 200 were involved in this demonstration; that of the nation's 22-odd million black citizens, 200 were involved in the race riot, and of the vast number of people in the country who want peace, only 100 were at the peace demonstration—all that goes by the board. (Nevertheless, the demonstrations against Nixon continued. When, in March 1974, he appeared at an "Honor America" rally in Huntsville, Alabama, before an audience carefully calculated to be favorable to him, he was greeted by demonstrators carrying signs reading "Honor America—Impeach Nixon!") [2]

Finally, television gives the viewer no chance to go back in his own mind. With a newspaper, a magazine, or a book, if what is happening is complicated, it is possible to reflect on it, then go back and read it a second or third time. In television, normally, the viewer gets it the first time or not at all.

Notwithstanding all these defects in the information system, on the part of both the government and the media, there are plusses to be thankful for.

There *are* forces at work attacking the government's mania for secrecy, of which the Senate Watergate hearings were the most conspicuous recent evidence.

Newspapers, though their one-city-one-newspaper concept is most invidious, are certainly more responsible than they were even a generation ago; and television, though by its very nature it probably never can become the perfect medium, at least gives evidence of recognizing its shortcomings.

All this does not satisfactorily answer the question of the public's dilemma, but here the great advantage lies in the very mass of informational material available. If the local newspaper has its defects, there are always the news magazines. If television allows no time for serious reflection, there are always books. And if books and magazines are too expensive, there is always the public library.

So, for the young citizen today, there certainly can be no lack of information on which to base his judgment. It is all there, for the viewing and the reading. But it must be *used*. Said James Madison: "Knowledge will forever govern ignorance. And a people who mean to be their own governors must arm themselves with the power knowledge gives . . ." [3]

As Bacon said, "Knowledge itself is power." [4]

NOTES

CHAPTER ONE

1. *New York Times*, September 23, 1973

2. Quoted in *The Life and Selected Writings of Thomas Jefferson*, edited by Adrienne Kock and William Peden (Modern Library, 1944).

3. Speech in Moscow, 1920, cited by H. L. Mencken in *A New Dictionary of Quotations* (Knopf, 1942).

4. *The Chinese, Their History and Culture* by Kenneth Scott Latourette, 4th edition (Macmillan, 1971).

5. From the First Phillipic

6. Volume I of Modern Library edition, 1935.

7. *Milton* by Hilaire Belloc (Lippincott, 1935).

8. *Freedom of the Press from Zenger to Jefferson*, edited by Leonard W. Levy (Bobbs-Merrill, 1966).

9. *New York Times*, July 1, 1971

10. Article on Waterloo by A. F. Becke in *Encyclopaedia Britannica*.

11. *Roosevelt and Hopkins* by Robert E. Sherwood (Harper, 1948).

12. *The Life of Reason: I-Reason in Common Sense* by George Santayana; one-volume edition revised by Daniel Cory (Scribner, 1953).

CHAPTER TWO

1. *A Thousand Days* by Arthur M. Schlesinger, Jr. (Houghton Mifflin, 1965).

2. These facts about the Watergate case are taken from the *New York Times Sunday Magazine* section of July 22, 1973, which was entirely devoted to the topic.

3. *New York Times*, September 5, 1973

CHAPTER THREE

1. *Inside the Third Reich* by Albert Speer (Macmillan, 1970).

2. *History of the Second World War* by B. H. Liddell Hart (Putnam, 1971).

3. *The Second World War* by Winston Churchill, Vol. II (Houghton Mifflin, 1967).

4. *The American Pageant* by Thomas A. Bailey, 3rd edition (Heath, 1966), reprinted from *A Book of Americans* by Rosemary and Stephen Vincent Benet (Rinehart, 1933).

5. In a letter to Charles Yancey, 1816, in *Life and Selected Writings of Jefferson op. cit.*

CHAPTER FOUR

1. *John Kennedy, a Political Profile* by James MacGregor Burns (Harcourt, 1960).

2. *The World of Swope* by E. J. Kahn, Jr. (Simon and Schuster, 1965).

3. *The Correspondent's War* by Charles H. Brown (Scribner, 1967).

4. *Ibid.*

5. *Ibid.*

6. *Ibid.*

CHAPTER FIVE

1. *The Bill of Rights, Its Origins and Meaning* by Irving Brant (Bobbs Merrill, 1965).

2. *New York Times*, January 28, 1973

CHAPTER SIX

1. *New York Times*, June 12, 1973

2. *New York Times*, February 11, 1973

CHAPTER SEVEN

1. *In Their Place: White America Defines Her Minorities*, edited by Lewis H. Carlson and George A. Colburn (Wiley, 1972).

2. *Ibid.*

3. Column by William V. Shannon in *New York Post*, September 23, 1957.

4. HR 18941 introduced August 12, 1970 by Representative Michael A. Feighan, D., Ohio.

5. For a full and cogent discussion of this problem see *Freedom of the Press—for Whom?* by Jerome A. Barron (Indiana University Press, 1973).

CHAPTER EIGHT

1. At the Foreign Policy Association, December 11, 1972.

2. *New York Times*, February 11, 1973

3. *Mandate for Change* by Dwight D. Eisenhower (Doubleday, 1963).

4. *New York Times*, April 9, 1973

5. *Ibid.*

6. *New York Times*, March 4, 1973

7. *New York Times*, July 1, 1973

8. *Time*, March 5, 1973

9. *New York Times*, March 15, 1973

10. *New York Times*, March 4, 1973

11. *New York Times*, February 25, 1973

12. *New York Times*, December 20, 1972

13. *Ibid.*

14. *Ibid.*

15. *Newsweek*, March 11, 1974

CHAPTER NINE

1. *The Press* by A. J. Liebling, 2nd edition (Ballantine, 1964).

2. *Newsweek*, March 4, 1974

3. Cited by Anthony Lewis in column "Privilege and Power," *New York Times*, August 20, 1973.

4. *Religious Heresies* by Francis Bacon, cited in *The Oxford Dictionary of Quotations* (Oxford University Press, 1955).

INDEX

175

ABOUT THE AUTHOR

Graduate of the Boston Latin School and Harvard College, Joseph Carter has been a writer and editor for most of his adult life. He has also been information officer for a number of government departments. This dual career, from both sides of the fence, so to speak, has provided a solid background for the writing of *Freedom to Know.*

Mr. Carter began his career as a newspaper reporter in Quincy, Mass., moved on to a Boston paper, and then spent five years in the army during World War II. After the war he was, for four years, a rewrite man for the *New York Herald Tribune.* This was followed by four years as information officer in various parts of the world for the Economic Co-operation Administration (the Marshall Plan), and further editorial stints at the *Herald Tribune* and *Atlas* magazine.

The author has written about 200 articles and short stories for well-known magazines and a number of books on various subjects.

Joseph Carter is married, has two daughters and two sons, and lives in Westport, Conn.

182